MUSKY MASTERY

THE TECHNIQUES OF TOP GUIDES

Featuring the tactics of:

**JOE BUCHER • GEORGE LANGLEY • PETE MAINA • STEVE HERBECK
ROGER SABOTA • GENE CURTIS • DAVE DORAZIO • BRIAN LONG • PETER HAUPT
BRUCE SHUMWAY • DICK MOORE**

by
Steve Heiting

Published by

 krause
publications

700 East State St.   Iola, WI 54990

Library of Congress Catalog Number: 91-77559
ISBN: 0-87341-198-6
Printed in the United States of America

CONTENTS

Dedication 4

Introduction 5

Chapter 1 — Flyfishing With George Langley 8

Chapter 2 — Jigs and Reapers With Gene Curtis 25

Chapter 3 — Surface Baits With Roger Sabota 40

Chapter 4 — Twitching With Pete Maina 52

Chapter 5 — Bucktails With Dick Moore 64

Chapter 6 — Night Fishing With Joe Bucher 76

Chapter 7 — Trolling With Brian Long 93

Chapter 8 — Jerk Baits With Dave Dorazio 104

Chapter 9 — Vertical Jigging With Bruce Shumway 116

Chapter 10 — Crankbaits With Peter Haupt 127

Chapter 11 — Sucker Fishing With Steve Herbeck 139

Epilogue 153

Author's Biography 156

Dedication

To my wife, Connie, for her support during the writing of this book and her understanding of my musky fishing fever, and to my late grandfather, Bernard Heiting, who introduced me to the greatest sport there is, fishing.

Introduction

Driving home from a visit at my in-laws' on New Year's Day 1991, I gradually tuned out the kids by pondering a desire I had entertained for the past month or so. Having written for magazines and newspapers for nearly a decade since my graduation from college, I wanted to take my writing career to another level: I wanted to author a book.

I knew full well that the best books are written by authors who sincerely love what they are writing about, especially if they can gather knowledge from true experts in the subject. Being an outdoor writer and a musky fanatic, I had always wanted to write a book about the big fish, but I was wary of the number of other books on the market.

Several books have been written by musky guides, and while there is much knowledge contained within those books' pages, the writing quality always left something to be desired. A few musky books have been penned by outdoor writers, and while they were well-written, the authors based their assumptions on their own experiences rather than those of true experts in the musky fishing field.

Then it hit me. What if I were to write a "how-to" musky book, combining the knowledge of some of the best musky fishermen alive today with my experience as an interviewer and writer? The book would be broken down into 11 chapters, one for each way of catching muskies, from flyfishing to bucktails to jerk baits to baiting with suckers. In each case, I would fish with the expert during the time of year his technique is at its best, learn from him first-hand how he goes about catching muskies with that technique, and then discuss what happened those days to make each chapter more entertaining.

Certainly the book would be different from any previously published, I figured. So, I bounced the idea off my wife, Connie. After she directed her attention from the kids to me, she agreed that it would be a great book. A few days later I contacted a publisher, who agreed there would be a market of fishermen looking for just such a musky book, perhaps the ultimate musky book.

The fishermen contacted to help with the book are all guides, people who spend nearly every day of the season on the water in the pursuit of muskies. Each one is an expert in the particular technique with which he was asked to help. There were many good guides who were not contacted for this book, but I wanted fishermen who would absolutely be the most knowledgeable for each respective chapter. They, too, saw the value of such a book and readily agreed to help out.

Each of the guides who was interviewed has personally caught or guided clients to muskies weighing in excess of 36 pounds, and seven of the 11 are responsible for the capture of fish weighing 40 pounds or more. Roger Sabota personally caught two 40-plus-pound fish within nine days of the other. And two of the anglers — Joe Bucher and Pete Maina — have caught or guided people to an unthinkable total of more than 200 legal-sized muskies in a year's time, and Maina had done it for two years running entering the 1991 season. (As it turned out, he made it three years in a row in 1991.)

Certainly, the credibility of the musky fishermen could not be doubted. The challenge before me was to corral the thoughts and knowledge of these men within the limited confines of a book chapter, while capturing as much as possible the flavor of the day in which we fished together.

It was a challenge I could not pass up.

Chapter 1

Flyfishing with George Langley

"God, I love muskies!"

I turned to see George Langley looking skyward, shouting his feelings about the battle that was going on. Myself? Sure, I love muskies, too, but the muscles in my forearm and wrist were screaming otherwise.

Tethered to the other end of nine feet of fly rod and a seemingly light line was a musky we hadn't yet seen, even though the battle was now more than 10 minutes long. The fish was powerful, staying well beneath the lake surface in spite of the constant pressure the long rod and I were applying.

"Get away from that motor!" I screamed at the fish as I tried to turn it from the back of the boat. It responded by diving beneath the boat hull, and I plunged the rod tip into the water to keep the line from fraying on the boat's bottom.

Though my mind was occupied with the thoughts of somehow subduing this musky, I couldn't help but think back to what George had told me when I booked this trip to go flyfishing for muskies.

"You talk about the ultimate catch and release method of catching muskies," George had said. "Even a 36-inch fish is going to give you a 20-minute fight. And when you're done, the fish is going to be tired, but all it's going to have is a single hook hole somewhere in its mouth. You're going to have the thrill of your life with a fish we'd consider small on conventional tackle, and then when you put it back the fish is going to be none the worse for wear."

That's fine, I mused. Sure the fish is going to survive. But will I?

The date was May 7, 1991, and I was well into the first day of my season-long quest to learn from the best sources possible the 11 different ways a musky can be caught. I had booked trips with a different guide for each technique, guides who are arguably the best the musky-rich state of Wisconsin has to offer.

When I called George to set up a date to go flyfishing, I was surprised that he wanted to go fishing early in the year. May 7 is well in advance of the regular musky opener in Wisconsin, which is always Memorial Day weekend. He said flyfishing was a deadly early season technique and we'd fish on Wisconsin-Michigan border lakes, where the musky season opens the first Saturday in May.

George owns Eagle Sports Center in Eagle River, Wisconsin, certainly one of the finer sport shops in an area well-known for lakes heavily infested with muskies. We met at Eagle Sports and then drove north to Lac Vieux Desert, a giant lake in extreme northern Wisconsin that features the early opener. Jokingly and somewhat lovingly referred to as "The Desert" by frustrated musky anglers, the big lake has earned its reputation as a producer of big fish.

May 7 was nasty by anyone's standards. Fast moving squalls spit snow flurries periodically from a leaden sky, and a series of cold fronts had caused the water temperatures to plunge as much as seven degrees in less than a week. "I just hope this weather didn't cause the fish to move out of the shallows," George wished.

George got his answer in a hurry. To show me how flyfishing is done, he took the rod first and expertly tossed the large streamer fly despite the strong wind. Standing in the bow of his custom-designed Ranger Fisherman boat, he suddenly snapped the long rod upward to set the hook. "There's one already," he spoke excitedly. Remarkably, we were still within sight of the boat landing.

While I worked my cameras George basically held on while the musky had its way for the early going of the fight. "Do you see what I mean?" he laughed as the fish — which was just shy of the legal minimum size of 32 inches — gave a spirited and powerful battle. When George finally reached into the water and grabbed the musky by the back of the head to unhook it, he grinned at me with one of those "I told you so" smiles.

Why is a musky fisherman and guide of George's stature — a person who has caught a 40-pound musky, guided a client to a 40-pounder, and has dozens of 30-plus pounders to his credit — so excited about fish the size most musky nuts wouldn't give a second look? Just hook a musky on a fly rod and find out.

George has personally taken muskies weighing up to 26 pounds on flyfishing gear, an event he fondly recalls as perhaps the highlight of his fishing career. And he has a dream of someday getting a 30-pounder — generally considered to be the measure of a true trophy muskellunge — on a fly rod. "That would be the ultimate," he smiled.

George Langley displays the business end of his flyfishing rig — a streamer tied to resemble a redtail chub, and a shock tippet of Mason Hard Line.

George gives credits to two people for inspiring him to fish muskies with a fly rod — his late grandfather, Fred Schunk of Waunakee, Wisconsin, who a friend once referred to as "an otherwise responsible banker who corrupted a perfectly normal child (George) into a lifetime of fishing"; and Larry Dahlberg, a member of the *In-Fisherman* magazine and television staff whose pioneering work with fly rods has conquered hundreds of large northern pike and "planted the seed" in George's mind.

"There are a lot of guys, including myself, who have caught big northerns on flies and Larry is perhaps the best. I figured if they can catch all those northerns on fly rods, I can catch a musky on fly gear, too," George recalled.

"I regard it as a frontier, one of the few frontiers remaining in musky fishing," George smiled. "It takes a 36-inch musky and turns it into an experience with a capital E. I've accounted for over 1,000 legal muskies but every fly rod fish still leaves my hands shaking."

Flyrodding for muskies is a spring and summer technique, though George wishes he could stretch it into a season-long tactic. "My two favorite ways to catch muskies are flyfishing in the spring and with suckers in the fall. I call them my two 'bookends' to the rest of the season."

Basically, flyrodding is an offshoot of the long-practiced twitching technique that has proven so deadly on spring muskies. In twitching, an angler lip hooks a four- to seven-inch long redtail chub and casts it with medium-weight spinning gear to the places muskies spawn — shallow, muck bottom bays where slow-moving creeks feed a lake. In fact, George uses streamer flies tied to resemble creek chubs and by slowly stripping them toward the boat, closely imitates the twitching action.

Flyfishing is generally thought of as the way to catch trout —

but musky flyfishing gear barely resembles the buggy-whip rods used by trout purists. George's equipment is specialized, and all first-rate so far as quality.

For a rod, George uses a 9-1/2-foot nine-weight Fenwick customized with an additional foregrip and a fighting butt. The foregrip eases the pressure on his wrist while fighting a fish, while the fighting butt allows him to jam the rod into his belly for leverage when he's getting tired. "It's so I can survive when I hook my 50-pounder," he quipped.

On the rod he attaches a Scientific Anglers Series 200 fly reel, on which he loads nine-weight intermediate sinking line, which has the characteristics of floating line for casting purposes but still helps get the streamer fly beneath the water. He backs the fly line with 50 yards of 30-pound test line, something he considers essential. "A nice fish will get you into the backing in no time," he smiled. "And if they want more, you just have to chase them with the boat."

For a tippet, George uses 12-pound Berkley Trilene XT with a 15-pound test shock tippet of Mason Hard Line, a monofilament specially designed for commercial tuna fishermen to stand up to sharp teeth. When summer rolls around George doesn't switch to heavier tippets, even though the fish become more active due to higher water temperatures. "You don't need to go heavier because you can't pressure the fish any more with the long rod," he explained.

The baits he uses are simple but well-tied jumbo flies. In the spring, George uses streamers made to resemble creek chubs, and they continue to work as the season progresses. However, later in the year he'll start using giant Dahlberg Divers, a floating streamer that plunges underwater when stripped by the angler, and large, mouse-type bass surface bugs. For evening fishing, when the water's calm, the mouse-like bugs really come into their own.

*With sunlight illuminating his flyline, George Langley strips in
line to retrieve his streamer.*

The baits are retrieved with a technique known as "stripping." While holding the rod at the foregrip, the fly line is pinched firmly to the rod by the angler's forefinger. It is then pulled about a foot at a time with the other hand, causing a stop-and-go retrieve muskies often find irresistible — similar to the retrieve of a jerk bait.

George also considers his boat part of his equipment. Only one flyrodder at a time can fish effectively, and this person takes a place in the bow of George's Ranger boat. You won't find any equipment, such as trolling motors or Anchor Mates, in the bow of George's boat, for any unusually-shaped object

Shorebound shot of George Langley, with his flyline illuminated by the sun, as he casts to a downed tree.

can easily become tangled with extra fly line hanging beneath the fly rod. A second angler is responsible for controlling the boat with a stern-mount trolling motor, but can fish with a spinning rod using the twitching technique described earlier. "The two techniques complement one another nicely," George noted. "You can only cast a fly so long before you tire, so it's great to switch off to spinning gear while your partner tries the fly rod."

George takes two approaches to flyfishing for muskies — spray casting and sight casting. In spray casting, the flyfisher casts in areas known to harbor muskies when spotting them isn't possible. "You do it early in the year, especially in darker waters, and later in the year when casting over weedbeds," he explained.

Sight casting is similar to bonefishing in the Florida Keys, George said, a practice that requires patience and stealth. "You have to be good with a fly rod, you have to spot the fish, stalk them with the boat, and then lay the fly right in front of them and hope they take it," he said. "Not only can you do this in the creek mouths at the beginning of the year when the water is clear, but later in June I'll fish deep, clear water lakes by sight casting to post-spawn fish. These lakes won't be as advanced as a shallow water lake and the fish will be in the spawning areas longer."

Flyfishing is a deadly clear water lake technique, George feels, because even the splash of a small bucktail landing nearby may alert a musky and increase its wariness. "A fly just isn't going to do that," he said.

Muskies seldom will follow a streamer to the boat, George has found. "It's not big enough to interest them in anything but eating," he said. "When it's in front of them, they either take it or ignore it."

When a musky takes a streamer, it's not the explosive strike

George Langley sets the hook into a musky.

one might expect. Instead, it's more of a stoppage of the bait, where the angler might feel a tick on the line or may think he's hung up on a weed. "They like to move in right behind it and suck it in. The fish are almost always hooked right in the mouth," George explained.

Though muskies hooked on a fly rod will jump, their fight is commonly a power struggle. The long rod pressures them upward, and their first instinct is to pull downward, away from the pressure. "Muskies have a reputation as being a fish that fights spectacularly but not for a long time. That reputation is very wrong," Langley feels. "The heavy tackle we use to throw the standard musky lures just doesn't give them a chance. But hook them on light stuff, like flyfishing gear...."

This I was experiencing first-hand with the musky I hooked at the beginning of this chapter. The nice fish — we knew it

George Langley hangs on while his musky struggles against the long fly rod.

George Langley's just-under-legal musky wallows next to the boat.

was no monster, but it was a healthy musky nonetheless — wasn't about to surrender to the fly rod and was giving a good account of itself in spite of the cold water temperatures.

For much of the day I had let George do the flycasting, basically because I hadn't tossed a fly in years and wanted to watch an expert at work. And work it was for me, though George made the technique look ridiculously easy — I figured I needed more practice.

In fact, twitching redtail chubs had put me onto one legal musky, though it was not well-hooked and shook off shortly after the fight began. But after lunch and as the day waned, I

A closeup of the author's 39-inch musky and the streamer used to catch it.

figured I might as well have another go at it with the fly rod. George was happy to turn the rod over, since his shoulder was already tiring from several hours of casting. "I'm going to ask my wife for a backrub tonight, but she'll just say I was out having fun," he smiled.

Just when I began to feel my shoulders growing tired — after only 15 minutes of casting — the streamer fly stopped as if snagged on a weed. But I set the hook anyway, just as George had instructed, and found myself linked to a feisty fish.

Each time I tried to lift the fish toward the surface where we could see it, the musky powered back to the bottom. Occasionally we caught a glimpse of its side flashing in the turbid water, but never did we get a good view of how big it was. George guessed it was a spawned-out female musky, since

The author's 39-inch musky and the equipment used to catch it.

*Eagle River Guide George Langley proudly holds up the author's
39-inch musky for a photo.*

males seldom grow to the size of this fish, and estimated its length at around 40 inches.

Then the fish started rolling in the tippet, and I got a good look at the beast that had so abused my forearm and wrist muscles during the lengthy battle. Sure, I've landed plenty of 40-inch and bigger muskies on conventional musky tackle, but never had I caught a musky of this size on such light gear.

Then something strangely wonderful began to happen — my hands began to shake with excitement, just as George said they would.

Finally, the fish lay near the surface, and by lifting on the

A selection of George Langley's favorite bugs and streamers used to catch muskies on flyfishing gear. The long bait in the middle is a Dahlberg Diver.

long rod I was able to unroll the musky from the line. George quickly slid his hand into its gill cover (he prefers to hand-land all fly-caught muskies rather than net them) and hoisted a long, green, absolutely beautiful fish into the boat.

Immediately the fish went into the Ranger's big livewell and George unhooked the fly from its mouth. He then closed the well's lid to allow me to set up my cameras, but not before making sure the musky would have no problem recovering in the aerated water.

My hands continued to shake as I fumbled with my camera gear. I tried to express my exact feelings to George but found myself stuttering with excitement. After getting the right lenses on the right cameras, we hurried to get the necessary photographs and then released the fish.

For the record, the musky measured 39 inches long, and probably weighed 15 or 16 pounds. For sheer excitement, it might as well have been a 30-pounder. Like George said, flyrod-caught muskies will do that to you.

To contact George Langley about a day of fishing, call him at (715) 479-8804.

Chapter Two

Jigs & Reapers with Gene Curtis

If ever there was a day for the Curtis Creature to shine, this was the day.

Conditions were far from perfect when Gene Curtis and I got together June 1, 1991 to fish with a technique he feels is far superior to anything else ever used for muskellunge — jigs and reaper tails.

"I can catch as many muskies on my jigs as anyone else can catch on bucktails and then some," Gene smiled as he kept his boat positioned along a weedline of Vilas County's North Twin Lake, in extreme northern Wisconsin.

Though Gene and I didn't catch any muskies on this day, I honestly feel it wasn't the technique — we did have a considerable amount of action and we each hooked and lost big muskies. While other anglers using other tactics were pulling their boats and heading to different water, Gene and I enjoyed a fairly busy day. We just couldn't put any of North Twin's finest in the boat.

"Boy, I wish we could get one of these things to open their mouth!" Gene growled as yet another musky followed to boatside but refused to hit. You could understand his frustration — already that week he and his clients had boated and released muskies measuring 44 and 39 inches from North Twin Lake, so he was conditioned to success. Both of those muskies were taken on Curtis Creatures, a bait of Gene's own design.

North Twin Lake is one of those places every musky hunter should visit at least once in his or her lifetime. A giant at about 2,800 acres, it can be difficult to fish the first few times on the water. But once you learn it, the lake's assortment of structure, such as rock bars and weedbeds, gives an angler a seemingly endless number of places to fish. North Twin is clear, so you can see a musky following while still a long way off, yet not too clear to preclude good fishing during daylight hours.

The muskies in North Twin are exceptionally marked with pure white lower jaws and underbellies gradually darkening to sharply contrasting stripes on their sides. And they grow fat on the lake's abundant forage base, which includes ciscos, redhorse suckers, walleyes and panfish. In fact, the day I fished with Gene some walleye anglers enjoyed good success until a musky they estimated at 45 to 48 inches long swam by their boat with a two-pound walleye crossways in its mouth. They never had another bite at that spot.

The last few days of May were marked by a myriad of thunderstorms that dumped several inches of water on an already saturated northern Wisconsin. And the day before Gene and I fished together was one of the nastiest. We ventured onto North Twin faced with nearly-flat water, a somewhat bright

Vilas County Guide Gene Curtis casts a Curtis Creature to the muskies of North Twin Lake.

sky, and fish already turned off by the cold fronts that brought the storms 24 hours earlier. Though the walleyes were biting, the muskies were, at best, reluctant.

And still we had an enjoyable day, thanks to the Curtis Creature.

The Curtis Creature is such an odd-looking lure that even Gene can't describe what it is supposed to look like. It features a wide, swimming-style one-ounce jighead, a long black plastic tail tipped with a No. 4 or 5 Colorado spinner blade, and a pair of giant single hooks — a 7/0 size hook aiming upward, and a 6/0 stinger hook pointing down. "You know, I'm not sure what it resembles," Gene smiled. "There are crayfish in this lake, and maybe that's what the muskies think

Gene Curtis retrieves a Curtis Creature. Note how he watches his line for the sign of a bite.

it is. It could be an injured minnow, but then there are big leeches in this lake, too, and they might think that's what they're eating."

Whatever it looks like to muskies, the Curtis Creature and the big "reapers" used by other fishermen — long, eel-like plastic worms attached to heavy jigs — are probably effective because of the way they are fished, Curtis feels.

"It's actually the location of fishing within two or three feet of the bottom that is probably what makes it so effective," Gene explained. "It will actually be seen by both active and neutral fish. An active fish will chase a bait, but a neutral fish wants to grab its food without chasing it down.

"It's like an appetizer. Very easy, slow, a quick bite for a basically dormant fish. It's not something huge that the musky has to grab and kill in order to eat. And that's why it will work under all conditions. I've had days out here when it was just like fishing walleyes, we had so many bites. But the bait seems to be especially effective when you would swear there aren't any muskies in the lake when fishing other baits," Gene continued.

To many of the fishermen on North Twin June 1, that's probably just the way it seemed — as if the muskies had all been washed away by the heavy rains. "Are you doing any good?" Gene asked a nearby angler, a person he recognized as a North Twin regular.

"Haven't seen a fish," he called back. "And you?"

"We've seen some," Gene answered, modestly. Actually, at the time we were quite enthused with what had been going on.

Just moments before I had witnessed something I hadn't before seen — two muskies followed my Curtis Creature to boatside at the same time. And just minutes earlier Gene had set the hook on a solid fish that jolted his rod downward twice before coming off. "That was a big fish," Gene said sadly. "I

Gene Curtis casts to the muskies of North Twin Lake.

was waiting all day for that 'tick' of a fish grabbing the bait as it dropped, and I finally got it and I missed him." And an hour before I lost a good fish at mid-retrieve and missed a nicely marked 34-inch musky that grabbed the bait during a figure-eight.

Oddly enough, the three muskies we lost that day hit in three of the most common ways muskies grab Curtis Creatures and reapers. "Maybe 50 or 60 percent of your hits will come at the boat. Otherwise, you'll just feel a 'tick' as the bait drops, similar to how it feels when a walleye grabs a jig, or maybe your line will just move to the side and you won't feel anything. And sometimes you'll just tighten up your line and the fish will be there. Some of the biggest muskies I've caught I didn't know were on until I tightened the line, and they were just there," Gene explained.

The big fish I lost, and I sincerely believe it had to be over 40 inches long because it jolted me back when I set the hook, grabbed the Curtis Creature on the drop and I never felt a thing — at least not until I tightened the line. I felt a weight and set the hook hard only to have the rod yanked back toward the water as the fish shook its head. Then it was gone.

And the fish that struck at boatside hit in a way that seemed to typify the close-but-oh-so-far success of the day. I spotted the fish coming in from the right, and before I could figure-eight, it tried unsuccessfully to suck the Creature in. It then quickly followed the bait into the figure-eight and apparently latched on as I completed the first turn. At the time, I couldn't see the fish because of surface glare, and I never felt it take the bait. Gene and I surmised the musky moved the bait forward as it latched on and shook its head side-to-side, creating just enough slack so that I couldn't feel its weight or strike.

"He's got it! Hook!" Gene shouted. I followed his instructions but merely pulled the bait out of the water as the fish

Gene Curtis steers his Ranger boat toward a North Twin Lake hot spot.

returned to the depths.

Rule Number One. Muskies get off. Rule Number Two. It helps to cuss a little.

The way to fish Curtis Creatures and other jig-type musky lures is so demanding that concentration is of the utmost. Water clarity will determine the weed line in any northern lake, and Gene will position his boat right on the edge, which is typically in eight to 12 feet of water. He casts the weighted baits to the weed edge and lets them sink until they reach bottom — as indicated by a sudden slackening of the line. Gene points his rod tip at the bait and then rapidly cranks four or five revolutions on the reel handle before pausing to let the bait sink again. When the line goes slack as the bait finds bottom, he repeats the process.

Not once does Gene use his rod tip to "swim" the bait to the boat, instead preferring to do everything with the reel. It's a challenge to constantly be watching the line, waiting for it to go slack as the Creature hits bottom, or trying to feel the "tick" of a feeding musky.

Gene uses only high-quality equipment in the technique to maximize his fish catching ability. To the bait he attaches a 16-inch wire leader made of single strand 40-pound test piano wire, which efficiently cuts through weeds while preventing bite-offs from the muskies' sharp teeth. The leader is tied to 20-pound test Berkley TriMax photochromatic line, which glows sufficiently to allow easy line-watching.

"I know some guys use braided dacron line instead of mono. I've switched to dacron and back to mono many times. Every time I lose a couple fish that I blame on the line I'll switch," Gene said with a wry smile. "And no matter what you use, you've got to be able to see it, so that's why I use the photo-chromatic line. I wouldn't use it if I didn't like it."

Gene has found that a seven-foot graphite rod, like Cabela's

Fish Eagle, the St. Croix Premier or George Langley's Supreme models, will work best at casting and retrieving jig-type lures. And to these rods he attaches Garcia Ambassadeur reels in the 5500C or 5600C models, which he modifies by removing the anti-reverse mechanism.

"So many fish hit at boatside that I want to be in full control when that happens," he explained. "I'm prepared to give line in a hurry if I have to."

How Gene Curtis came to become a diehard jig fan is an interesting story. Back when he lived in Beloit, in extreme southern Wisconsin, he first learned of using jigs and reapers from members of the Flatlanders Chapter of Muskies, Inc. "There are a half-dozen guys there who are really dedicated reaper fishermen," he said.

Then, when Gene and his wife, Norma, purchased their present home on North Twin Lake, a friend gave him some reapers to try. "I rigged it on a rod and never used it all summer, until one day I grew tired of throwing my Eddie Bait (a big, gliding-style jerk bait). And you know, that took a lot because I caught a lot of fish on Eddie Baits over the years. So I threw the reaper and had a hit on the second cast. I thought I had a weed, but as I pulled it toward the boat it just kept going under it.

"That's how subtle these neutral fish are when they take a reaper. By the time I realized that I had a musky on the line it was gone. I never got a hook into it," he recalled.

After that episode, Gene became hooked, so to speak, on reaper fishing. And the first full year he used them he hooked and landed a 30-1/2-pounder that he had mounted. He's released every big musky since, and has caught a bunch of them on jig-type baits up to 35 pounds.

"The theory that jigs are a small fish bait is entirely wrong. I've released fish up to 35 pounds, and I've guided people to muskies weighing 38 pounds on jigs and reapers," he said. And not only do reapers produce big fish, but they also pay off in numbers. As a member of the Headwaters Chapter of Muskies, Inc., Gene tagged 170 muskies during 1990, including well over 100 fish measuring at least the legal minimum of 32 inches. He also finished tenth internationally in the Muskies, Inc., annual release contest that year with 44 legals.

Gene developed the Curtis Creature from the standard jig-and-reaper in an attempt to offer a change of pace to muskies that had already seen the usual fare and grown lure-shy. He

Gene Curtis proudly displays a 30-1/2-pound musky, a fish taken several years ago that proved to him the effectiveness of jig and reaper fishing.

Gene Curtis prepares to release a trophy musky caught on a Curtis Creature. (Photo courtesy Gene Curtis).

threads 20-pound test braided dacron through the plastic tail and ties on a snap swivel, to which he attaches the Colorado spinner blade.

"It's a different look. A lot of guys fish with jigs or reaper tails, but few fish reapers with spinners on them until they fish with me," he said.

All Curtis Creatures feature a black tail. "Black is beautiful, I guess," Gene quipped. He varies the color of the spinner blade, and has found silver to be especially effective on North Twin while a blade painted orange on one side and black on the other has been promising.

Though it seems *everyone* has heard of the Curtis Creature, not everybody owns one. Gene only produces about 500 a year, which are sold in George Langley's Eagle River, Wisconsin, sport shop, Eagle Sports Center. And they sell fast. "I sell as many as I can make. I could probably go fulltime into the lure business, but for one thing I'd hate to see a lot of

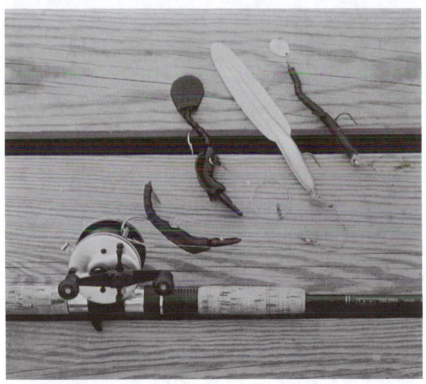

A few of Gene Curtis' favorite jig and reaper combinations. The Curtis Creature is attached to the rod.

Gene Curtis displays one of his famous Curtis Creatures.

other people using a bait that's been so effective for me," Gene said with a sly smile. "I'd also have to give up a lot of fishing time to make more."

Gene will stack his Curtis Creature against any other bait, on any day. He's had so much success with it under so many different conditions that it's basically all he'll fish with. "It can outfish a bucktail because it's more effective at 'straining' the water. You have to work a bucktail fast and keep on moving, while this method allows me to fish slowly and throw more casts on a given piece of structure. And in the fall, I like the Creature better than sucker fishing because it's easier for the muskies to grab than a big sucker. Remember one of these is a big bait anyway, and it's easy for a musky to take rather than having to hunt it down and kill it."

I believe him. Although bucktails and suckers and jerk baits belong in a musky hunter's arsenal, Gene and I had too much success on what should have been a lousy fishing day to doubt his word.

To contact Gene Curtis for a day of fishing, call him at (715) 545-4001.

Chapter Three

Surface Baits with Roger Sabota

Roger Sabota still trembles when he remembers the big musky he saw over a decade ago follow a surface bait to the side of his boat.

On Labor Day that year Roger was casting his favorite surface bait — a Snodlo — when the monster showed itself. "The wake behind the bait was so high it knocked the Snodlo off balance and it lost its action, and then of course the fish lost interest," Roger said. "It was just a huge, huge fish, closer to 60 inches than 50 inches. It was the color of a gunnysack with the profile of a bushel basket."

Roger never did catch that fish, the largest musky he's ever seen in the water. And nobody has seen that fish since some friends of Roger's hooked and lost it on a jerk bait, but he still feels excitement every time he casts a surface bait in the area the big fish lived. He swears by surface baits for muskies, and besides the follow from the giant, Roger has plenty of reason to have confidence in them. He's caught muskies as large as 36 pounds 10 ounces on the floating plugs and estimates over half of the fish topping 25 pounds that he and his guiding clients have caught have been lured by surface baits.

And that vote of confidence comes from a man who, a few years back, landed a pair of muskies that pulled the scales to the magical 40-pound barrier within a nine-day period. Those big fish weren't hooked on surface baits, but to Roger, it just doesn't matter.

"When I see a big fish come up behind the bait, speed up when I speed up the bait, and then smack it...well, it's just the most exciting fishing I do," he smiled. "I've had tremendous success fishing the surface, and my first big fish, that is over 30 pounds, came on the surface. I guess you can say I'm hooked."

Rhinelander, Wisconsin, guide Roger Sabota talked about his obsession with surface baits as we plied the waters of Boom Lake, actually a Wisconsin River flowage bordering on Roger's home city. Though conditions weren't right for catching muskies — a cold front had blown through overnight, leaving blue skies and puffy white clouds the order of the day — Roger and I pitched surface baits with confidence. We also tried other types of artificial lures, from twitch baits to bucktails to jerk baits, yet most of our action came on the surface. So we kept throwing the big, wooden, floating plugs.

The only fish caught that day, which was June 10, 1991, was a precocious northern pike that grabbed a surface plug a full fourth of its length. Yet every hour or so a musky would cruise in behind one of our baits, its snout just an inch or so from the tail hook — just close enough to make us wonder when one of the cursed things would open its cavernous mouth and grab the lure.

Roger's experience seems to contradict the beliefs of many musky anglers that surface baits are "small fish" lures. "That

"When I see a big fish come up behind the bait, speed up when I speed up the bait, and then smack it...well, it's just the most exciting fishing I do."

belief is totally unfounded," Roger explained. "But you've got to fish surface baits slow. Therein lies the secret to catching big fish. When the other guides in my guide group started throwing surface baits a few years back they retrieved them fast and caught a lot of small fish. But when we started slowing down...wow, what a difference. That's when we started getting the big ones."

About the time of year when Roger and I fished together is the time to start thinking about using surface lures, he explained. "I start using surface baits when I begin to see small ducks on the water. With a surface bait I'm trying to imitate something small on the surface, something such as a little duckling.

"Last year, about this time of June, I started watching one

Rhinelander, Wisconsin Guide Roger Sabota retrieves a surface bait across the top of Boom Lake.

43

duck family that had 12 ducklings. Every couple of days there was one fewer following the hen around the lake. When they finally were able to fly away, there were only three left. I guess they helped fatten up a couple of our Boom Lake muskies."

Sabota kept his boat near all types of cover — shoreline, points reaching out from the shore and midlake bars covered with cabbage. Most of the fish we raised were near midlake bars that had deep water nearby — classic musky water — though one fish tried to grab but missed one of Roger's plugs near a weedy shoreline. And then there was the fish that wasn't caught because, well, read on and find out.

It didn't really seem to matter what time of day it was, we just kept seeing fish follow our baits all day long.

"I've caught them on surface baits at all times of day, though I like low-light conditions like early or late in the day or on days that are hazy or raining, when there's little light penetration into the water. But contrary to what most people believe about when to use surface baits, we've caught them on the surface during the middle of the day and in all kinds of wind conditions. Really, the strength of the wind blowing only dictates the kind of lure to use," Roger noted.

When a chop breaks the surface, Roger uses surface plugs that churn the water and throw up some spray, like Topper Stoppers, Hi-Fin Double Teaser Tails and Hellraiser Cherry Twists. In calm conditions, you'll see Roger fishing with baits that have a more subtle action, like his favorite, the Snodlo, or Gooch's Tally Whackers and Mouldy's Hawg Wobblers. "Have you seen that new Magnum Hawg Wobbler?" he asked. "Boy, is that going to catch some big fish."

Roger's favoritism of the Snodlo is well-founded. One of the Snodlos he owns has 10 fish topping 25 pounds to its credit, and was the bait that lured the largest fish ever entered in the Minocqua World Musky Hunt — a 44-incher — for Roger's

Roger Sabota intently watches his surface bait as it nears his boat. (arrow)

client in 1990. Designed by Roger's late friend, David Snoddy, the bait is the finest-constructed the Rhinelander guide has ever seen.

"When they were made they were balanced so perfectly. Dave would even balance the bait for the type of rod and line test you were going to use," Roger recalled fondly. "I like to work the bait so that the tail just splashes back and forth and doesn't spin. It's a very difficult bait to use, but once you've mastered it it just looks so good coming across the surface of the water."

Roger prefers his surface baits to be black, and even if they are a different color he's spray-painted the belly with black paint. "When those muskies are looking up at the bait, I want a contrasting color against the sky. When I'm night fishing I definitely want a black bottom because the sky is the lightest thing the musky sees. And if I'm using a blade bait I want fluorescent blades for just that much more contrast."

Though Roger spends a great deal of time on Boom Lake with its tea-stained waters, he will even use fluorescent-colored blades on surface baits in clear water. "Again, I like the contrast," he explained.

Roger also believes in tuning each bait so that "it sounds right" as it crawls across the surface. Just how a bait is supposed to sound is a subjective thing that varies with the tastes of the individual angler. But he has one guide friend who has a secret to tuning baits. "He says he puts his beagle on the dock with him, and when the beagle starts whining when he's retrieving a bait he knows it's tuned properly," Roger smiled.

One of the ways that Roger "tunes" his baits is rather simple — he doesn't use a wire leader. "I haven't been bitten off, but I tell my customers that if they feel more comfortable with a wire leader to go ahead and use one. Surface baits just have more mass to them and that keeps the line away from the musky's teeth. Besides probably being visible to the muskies, I feel that extra weight on the nose of the bait caused by the wire leader throws them off-balance."

He uses a heavy-duty snap swivel to attach the bait to his line, which is DuPont Magnum 14/40 cofilament. "I always used black dacron but two years ago I went to monofilament and increased my action. I feel the DuPont cofilament does a good job of bridging the two types of line by having low visibility like mono and low stretch like dacron," he said.

For a rod, Roger uses St. Croix 7- or 7-1/2-footers. The long rod length helps keep most of the line out of the water during a retrieve, further improving the action of the surface baits, and helps with hook-setting by providing a long, sweeping action. On top of the rod Roger affixes an Ambassadeur bait-casting reel because he enjoys that make's durability.

Another reason for liking surface baits comes from Roger's profession as a fishing guide. "It's just a great bait for inexperienced clients. Even if they get a backlash, their bait won't sink and get hung up on the bottom," he said. "And it doesn't take much for a beginner to master a slow retrieve on the surface."

A good musky guide has plenty of stories, and one of Roger's favorites involves a youngster and his father who booked him for a day of musky fishing. "I gave the kid a Creeper, which works best when retrieved slowly, and you can cast it a hundred times and get a backlash on every cast and never lose it," Roger smiled. "Right away, the kid had a 37-inch fish hit the bait but he never hooked it and the fish just shook its head, got the kid wet with spray, and got off.

"Then, with musky fishing being what it is — hours of boredom separated by seconds of sheer terror — things got slow so I moved the boat to what I consider a big-fish bar. Suddenly the kid tries to pull his bait up from the water to cast and can't. I look at it," Roger continued, his voice rising with excitement, "and there's a 50- to 55-inch musky alongside the boat with its mouth closed on the bait. I yelled 'Jerk!' and the kid looked at me and said 'What?' and that big fish just shook its head and got off."

In both instances the youth had more than enough opportunity to hook a nice musky, and hooking fish on a surface bait is what Sabota calls a great challenge, even for experts. "I'm constantly telling clients to wait until they feel the weight of the fish, and this morning I pulled my Snodlo away from a fish," he laughed. "You've just got to wait until you feel that fish. You can't set the hook when you see the musky come up to take the lure, because you'll miss him every time."

Indeed, Roger did miss a musky on a surface bait that morn-

Roger Sabota's favorite surface baits are, from left: Snodlo, Cherry Twist, Hawg Wobbler, Topper Stopper, and Double Teaser Tail.

*"All of a sudden a fish hit out in the darkness with a 'Kawoosh!'
and all three of us set the hook and two baits came flying back at
us through the boat while one connected. Somehow, after we got
the baits all untangled we still caught the fish."*

ing. A 34- or 35-incher came in from the side and just as it was about to grab the bait...let's just say it didn't quite make it.

"I've screwed up with surface baits in every conceivable manner," Roger joked. "When I caught the 36-10 I had lost five fish in a row on surface baits, and they were all in excess of 30 pounds. When I hooked that 36-10 my buddy got the net and I said to him, 'Don't bother. I'm just going to lose it anyway.' I was gunshy.

"But it was good to lose all those big fish because that's how I got the Snodlo I've done so well with. I told Dave Snoddy about those fish and he said he'd make me one that hooked fish better, and he did."

And then another Sabota tale about surface baits and

Roger's best surface bait is this slow-moving Snodlo, which has accounted for ten muskies topping 25 pounds.

"missed" fish: "One night three of us were out musky fishing and all of us were using surface baits. All of a sudden a fish hit out in the darkness with a 'Kawoosh!' and all three of us set the hook and two baits came flying back at us through the boat while one connected. Somehow, after we got the baits all untangled we still caught the fish."

Theoretically, the best way to set the hook when a musky takes a surface bait is down and to the side, so that if a fish is missed the heavy plug doesn't come sailing back at the fisherman. "I know I've said that," Roger admitted. "But I set the hook upwards just like anyone else. I'm not worried about theory. I want to hook the fish."

Musky fishing being what it is, Roger and I didn't catch any muskies that day. Still, he shed some serious light onto a first-rate method to catch muskellunge, and more than proved his worth as a fishing guide by keeping me entertained when the fishing was slow. Heck, I'm ready to go back to Boom Lake for a shot at that 60-incher again.

To contact Roger Sabota for a day of fishing, call him at (715) 369-2283.

Chapter Four

Twitching with Pete Maina

"You know, it's really pretty when a couple of professionals get together. You really get to see how to handle fish."

The above statement was made in all mock seriousness by Pete Maina, a fishing guide from Hayward, Wisconsin. Sitting in the bow of the boat, with a towel pressed tightly to my thumb to stop the flow of blood, I cracked up.

My laughter was infectious and soon Pete, too, was roaring. It wasn't the first nor the last time we had to quit fishing that day because we were laughing so hard. After all, Pete is perhaps the most entertaining fishing guide in northern Wisconsin, and not just because he's a boatseat comedian. He's also extremely proficient at catching muskellunge, possibly the best ever.

During the 1990 fishing season Pete Maina and his clients

boated 214 legal-sized muskies. And to those who don't believe his figures, please understand that all of the fish Pete caught himself — over 130 legal muskies — were witnessed before they were released. Pete is quite active in the Hayward Lakes Chapter of Muskies, Inc., and through the 1990 season had won the master's release division three consecutive times after winning the men's division in 1987 and moving up.

Muskies, Inc. uses a scoring system giving an angler four points for each witnessed and released fish plus a point for each inch over 30 that the musky measures. For example, a 32-incher, the legal minimum in Wisconsin, would count as six points. Each year since he went on his recent musky-catching spree, Maina released well over 100 legal muskies, scoring some 1,000 points annually. Nobody in the history of Muskies, Inc., a group that includes some of the most hardcore musky anglers ever, has come close to matching Pete's figures.

And Pete's average was padded the day we fished together — July 18, 1991 — as he and I both released legal fish. Pete hooked and successfully landed a 36-inch battler, and I boated a 37-incher later that evening. It was my fish that caused my thumb to bleed, as a dagger-like tooth laid it wide open. Pete also knew pain that day as his three-footer jabbed him in two places and took an inch of skin off a knuckle. It was quite a spectacle.

The thrashing fish made us look like a couple of rookies.

Our success, and what eventually led to our painful hands, came from a technique called twitching. It's very similar to what bass fishermen have been doing with Rapalas for years — retrieving a floating-diving minnow bait with a pull-pause-pull-pause pattern. In the last few years twitching has taken the musky fishing world by storm, and Pete Maina has been at the forefront. To him, twitching is much more than a nervous condition.

Hayward, Wisconsin, Guide Pete Maina works a Grandma bait toward his boat. Note the fluorescent-colored bait in the water a short distance from the boat. (arrow)

"I've been twitching for seven years, but I have to give credit to my friend, Dick Minnick, who has been twitching Rapalas for over 25 years for muskies. He told me about it back before I started thinking for myself about fishing," Maina said. "After all, you jerk a jerk bait and you retrieve a bucktail, but these baits with 'tongues' (diving lips) on them...heck, you're supposed to just reel them in, aren't you? Sure they work that way, but they're just deadly when you twitch them.

"That wounded look twitch baits have to them is just dynamite. It triggers a fish to hit, rather than just follow the bait to the boat."

Pete and I were fishing Teal Lake, located northeast of Hayward along State Highway 77 in Sawyer County. It's one of the prettiest places in all of Wisconsin, and it offers some of the

"That wounded look twitch baits have to them is just dynamite. It triggers a fish to hit, rather than just follow the bait to the boat."

best musky and walleye fishing to be found anywhere. Maina probably knows Teal and connecting Lost Land Lake better than anyone, and you'd think for all the fish he's caught from them over the years he'd have them all named. However, there are so many muskies in this pair of lakes that it's hard to pinpoint any single fish; rather, you fish where you expect a bunch of muskies to be.

A huge thunderstorm had blown through that morning and the skies had since cleared. However, the heavy southwest winds brought heat with them, and a scorching 95-degree reading could be had from the deck of Pete's boat, a Tuffy Marauder. More storms were predicted for that evening, so just what the muskies were going to do would be anybody's guess.

Pete Maina maneuvers his boat toward shoreline cover.

Pete motored his boat within casting distance of small rock humps and bars in Teal Lake, which he prefers over Lost Land simply because of its varied structure. "An idiot can fish Lost Land," he feels. "You just park your boat on top of a weed flat and drift. Sooner or later you're going to get some action." But the muskies in Teal Lake, or at least the ones that live near the rock humps, weren't home, so we tried some weedy bays. It was in such a bay that I had a follow from an undersized musky, and oddly enough, it would be one of only two follows we'd have all day.

We then switched to shoreline cover, thinking maybe the fish would be located in the wood or downed timber. Pete turned the stern of the Marauder into the wind and slipped along the shoreline, using his Motorguide Backtroller trolling motor to control our speed.

"There's a fish!" Pete hissed suddenly, sweeping the Grandma Bait into a wide figure eight. "It was a fairly good one, too. I'd say it was about 37 inches long, but it stayed so deep." After four or five times around the figure eight Pete lifted the bait from the water and the musky, which had been hiding under the boat the entire time, swam out and back toward the shoreline.

"You son-of-a-gun," Pete complained, aiming a cast in the direction the musky was headed. No sooner had the bait plopped in the water than the musky grabbed it, tearing the surface to spray as it felt the sting of the hook.

After a brief but spectacular battle, the musky was at boatside, the fire tiger Grandma Bait embedded in the corner of its jaw. Pete lifted the spent fish into the boat, held it for a picture, quickly unhooked it and laid it against the four-foot ruler. As he moved to release it, twelve pounds of musky went berserk, slashing Pete with its teeth as it leapt from his hands and landed in the water. Not a pretty release, by far, especially

Pete Maina proudly displays his 36-inch musky before releasing it back to Teal Lake. Note the clipped fin — apparently this fish had been stocked by the Wisconsin Department of Natural Resources.

Just as he does with hundreds of muskies every year, Pete Maina releases his 36-incher to fight again. Just after the photo was taken, the musky thrashed and cut Pete's hand.

considering all the blood Pete lost, but still a release.

Somewhere around musky number sixty for Pete that year, he estimated. "I've got to look it up and see how well I'm doing," he said. "I'd hate to be having a better year than I think I'm having and then get lazy and not register a few fish."

As the day wore on and my skin grew a darker shade of red (Pete's got one of those tans that you only see in the old surfer movies), Maina had a chance to tell more about this deadly musky catching technique.

"Even though this is the middle of summer, spring and fall are really the best for twitching. Still, you have to keep twitching in mind during the summer because sometimes a hot twitch will work so much better than a bucktail. And you've got to remember that twitching will work anytime a musky wants to feed on a minnow-type critter because twitch baits seem to hook them so much better than most other baits."

Maina likes baits like Grandmas and Bagleys, smallish crankbaits that feature wide sides and have a slow wobble, rather than the tight wiggle of a Rapala. He keeps a wide selection of colors of all the baits in his boat, knowing that fluorescent colors work better in dark water and natural colors are tops in clear lakes.

He also likes divers, such as the Bucher Depth Raider, because of the depth control they afford. "With sharp snaps of the rod tip you can keep them just under the surface for half the retrieve, just so they're over the weeds. And then you can slam them down at the weed edge or in pockets so they dive, and this triggers fish that are waiting in ambush on the edges.

"That jointed Bucher Depth Raider...you can keep it just under the surface and then bust it down on the weedline. I've really had that work well for me on a lot of different lakes," he continued.

"Still, no matter what I'm throwing, I want to keep the bait just ticking the tops of the weeds. I'm a firm believer in ripping weeds and the triggering effect that will have on muskies." Depending on the bait and weed depth, Maina will jerk his rod tip either upward or downward to impart the twitching action.

Time of day doesn't really matter, Maina believes, but then he doesn't believe in "time of day" theories for any bait. "A musky's going to eat what he wants when he wants, no matter when it is," he said.

If there is a time not conducive to twitching, it's after a big cold front, Pete feels. Then, he just uses a straight retrieve to bring the crankbait to the boat.

The back of Pete's boat is replete with gear, much of it designed for twitching. For this technique, he prefers Quantum

Pro 1 reels mounted on Quantum seven-foot graphite rods. "The long rod gives the bait better action and it's more versatile for keeping the bait up high over the weeds," he explained. "Long rods have become the rage for musky fishing because they allow for a more sweeping hookset and are more forgiving when a fish is thrashing. Those are great advantages, but the longer rods seem to be designed for twitching."

Pete uses Berkley 30-pound test braided dacron for most applications, but when using six-inch baits, like the Grandma lure, he goes to 20-pound test monofilament. To the business end he attaches a 27-pound test single strand wire leader. "The light leader prevents cutoffs while allowing the baits better action," he noted.

All the advice in the world about twitching for muskies, from equipment to actual technique, didn't matter one bit to the musky I caught later that day. After Pete's fish we hit a lull and didn't even see a follow during the next four hours of casting. Of course, even the best musky fishermen can't get the fish to bite when they don't want to. Even the distant rumbling of thunder and the gradual clouding of the sky didn't seem to have an effect.

Until 8:30, that is. Pete and I continued casting the shorelines and I varied my technique to slow down the action of my six-inch Grandma Bait. I was using a fire tiger pattern because of the combination of dark water and darkening skies, twitching the bait ever-so-slowly so it just dove beneath the surface before I let it rise to break the surface again. This methodical retrieve was more than one musky could take.

The fish simply rolled up out of three feet of water and literally ate the Grandma Bait, and when I instinctively snapped the tip of my seven-foot St. Croix rod to set the hook, the musky's ample white belly bulged the surface. Then it charged the boat, a well-known musky trick to get slack line and dislodge the lure. Its head-shaking run took it past the bow of the Tuffy and out into deeper water, taking line against my lightly-set drag.

After pausing for a moment in about eight feet of water, the musky tried to gain leverage by working beneath the 17-foot fiberglass boat. I plunged the rod tip into the water and walked it around the back of Pete's 60-horsepower Evinrude, ever mindful that any edge of the lower unit or the propeller could slice the line cleanly.

Then it was over. The musky came up to the boat and rolled on its side, a sure sign its fight was complete. I handed Pete my rod and set up the camera, then traded camera for rod to unhook the musky and hold it for a picture.

Yet the musky had other ideas. It let me ease it onto Pete's four-foot measuring stick, and we noted that the lower lobe of its caudal fin just touched the 37-inch line. I lifted the musky up and removed two hooks from its face, then turned my attention to the treble lodged in the corner of its jaw. "I could have let this one swim around until next June and he never would have gotten away," I remarked to Pete, who was patiently waiting for me to remove the hooks before he started snapping photos.

Finally, the last hook popped free from the musky's mouth. All 37 inches of fish then celebrated its freedom by thrashing wildly, flopping from my fingers and back into the water. Pete never snapped a photo; I guess he was being entertained too well. Anyway, as the fish gained freedom one of its teeth caught the edge of my thumb, leaving a three-quarter-inch gash too deep for me to dare looking at.

When our laughter subsided and I started to get over the pain that was throbbing from the side of my thumb down into my wrist, it dawned on me how lucky we'd been to get pictures of Pete's fish. "Boy, am I glad we didn't have to rely on that

Pete Maina's favorite twitching baits include: top — Bucher Depth Raider; second row — Bagley Bang-O-B, Bomber Long- A; third row — Bucher Depth Raider, six-inch Grandma, bottom — nine-inch Grandma.

fish for photos for this chapter," I smirked, and Pete again joined me in some serious giggling.

That's when he sprang the deadpan comment about how "beautiful" it was to watch a couple of pros handle fish.

When I woke the next morning my sides ached, and it didn't take me long to realize why. In fact, I thought back to the 37-incher flying from my hands back into the water, and started to laugh again.

Ouch.

To contact Pete Maina for a day of fishing, call him at (715) 462-3952.

Chapter Five

Bucktails with Dick Moore

The Minocqua Chain of Lakes has earned a reputation over the years as a top musky producer, and its legend goes back to the turn of the 20th century when two fisheries crew members supposedly netted a 102-pound musky from its waters.

Today the famous Minocqua Chain, which is located in Oneida County, Wisconsin, draws people from across the Midwest to boat its clear waters. But for the musky angler who is caught up with the tradition and the history of the Chain, fishing with Dick Moore is recommended. He's a fisherman's tour guide.

"Over there, that's where Ray Kennedy (a famous Minocqua guide, whose father, E.D. Kennedy, was involved with the alleged 102-pounder) caught his 50-pounder...."

"It was along this shoreline where the DNR was netting spawning fish and we were watching from a distance. Then they motioned us over to look at this huge, huge walleye that they'd caught. They asked my daughter to hold it for a picture. You know, that fish was 44 inches long...."

"My family was camping here on Lake Tomahawk when we heard that my friend Gene Allen caught his 51-pounder (the largest musky caught by hook and line in Wisconsin for many years, taken in 1975). When we heard Gene got the fish we had to go up there (to the Lac du Flambeau area, where he had caught the fish) and see it. We found Gene in a bar, and by then he could hardly stand up.

"Was that a long night...."

Well, you get the picture. Dick knows the names of the famous bars and points of the Minocqua Chain, but he prefers to remember them by the fish they've produced. And they've produced a lot of fish, not only for the people of the Woodruff-Minocqua area but for Dick himself.

And for as well as he knows the Minocqua Chain, Dick Moore knows an effective method for catching muskies. It's one that's practiced by all musky anglers at some time or another — bucktails — and is arguably the favorite technique of most musky hunters.

Chances are you own a bucktail tied by Dick Moore. True, it might not bear the name of "Musky-Teer" or "King Tut" or one of the other baits in his catalog, but he still may have tied it. Not only does his company, Moore's Lures, produce its own line of bucktails, but the company has tied tails for nearly every bucktail "manufacturer" in the market at one time or another.

Dick became so busy with his lure-making business that he gave up a successful guide career in 1986 for lack of time. Today, Dick works fulltime in Woodruff, but spends his evenings in the basement of his home near Mid Lake with his wife, Caryl, and a few part-timers tying bucktails and jigs.

It's an understatement to say that Dick knows bucktails. He

Heavy rain clouds darken the sky as lure manufacturer Dick Moore fishes Lake Tomahawk, casting and retrieving what he considers the top musky catching bait — a bucktail.

personally makes thousands of them every year and, after all, they are his favorite bait. "The real reason we use bucktails is, let's face it, there isn't a bait that is as easy to work or hooks a fish better than bucktails," Dick told me from the bow of his boat.

Out on the expansive waters of Lake Tomahawk on July 26, 1991, it might as well have been night — thunderstorms had rolled through northern Wisconsin all day. The temperature was cooling somewhat as a cold front began to move through, and I snapped an Eddie Bait onto the end of my line, feeling the muskies would not want to chase a bucktail given the conditions. Dick, of course, closed the snap of his wire leader on a bucktail.

On my fourth cast of the afternoon a nice musky in the three-foot-long range cruised in behind my Eddie, but refused to strike. Then Dick had a follow from a tiger musky (a musky-northern pike hybrid) that he judged was about 34 or 35 inches long. "I thought I'd get him to hit it," Dick muttered as he picked the bait from the water. "He was right behind it and looked like he wanted to eat. He just didn't."

After quickly coming in contact with those two active fish, Dick and I couldn't find any more muskies. We fished rock bars, gravel and sand bars, weed edges, and shoreline weeds. We tried shallow water and deep. I switched baits constantly, looking for the magic I knew probably wasn't going to happen. After all, the temperature was dropping even further as the cold front progressed.

Dick kept plugging away with the same nickel-bladed, red-tailed bucktail, exhibiting undaunting confidence. Finally, he had a strike near a shoreline weedbed and boated an undersized musky, which proved to be the only musky we caught that day.

With such little activity from the muskies, Dick had plenty

of time to fill me in on why he considers bucktails THE bait for muskellunge. The one thing he hasn't discovered in over 25 years of making bucktails is the answer to the question musky anglers have been asking for as long as there have been bucktails — why muskies eat them when they don't resemble anything in the food chain.

A typical bucktail has a blade that revolves around a straight wire shaft, a series of brass or plastic beads threaded onto the shaft for a "body," and at least one treble hook covered with deer tail hair or marabou at the rear. Then there are spinner baits, which look like giant, open safety pins with a large jig at the bottom and a spinner blade at the top. About the only way to fish either type of spinner is to cast them out and reel them in with a steady retrieve, which causes the blade to spin around the shaft and the tail to flutter somewhat. Of course, there are variations to these descriptions, but Dick has yet to see a fish or a critter swimming in any of his favorite lakes that looks anything like a bucktail.

"It just has to be the vibration of the blade," Dick reasoned. "I don't think any of us know what triggers them to hit a bucktail. I don't think that they're hungry or feeding, they just seem to want to hit bucktails. And I don't think it has so much to do with the hair on the bucktail, since I do well in dirty water and after dark with them. It's got to be the blade's vibration.

"In fact, I think you could do just as well with a bucktail that has no tail, that is in fact just a straight spinner. But I can't sell them that way because nobody would buy them."

The type of blade to use varies with the different applications, Dick explained. Essentially, there are three blade types — Colorado, French, and willow leaf. The Colorado blade is a large, rounded blade that provides lift and is effective in shallow water when fishing over weeds. This style is at its best in dark water because the heavy vibrations it gives off signals muskies from a long ways. The French blade, which is oval-shaped, is a good all-purpose blade and can be fished at almost any depth, while the willow leaf, which is, of course, shaped like a willow leaf, provides little lift and allows a bucktail-using angler to fish deeper water.

"Ninety percent of the time my favorite bucktails have a French blade on them," Dick said. "I can use it in almost any condition, but the muskies really seem to go for it. If I had to

"I don't think any of us know what triggers them to hit a bucktail. I don't think that they're hungry or feeding, they just seem to want to hit bucktails."

pick one bucktail to use all day, I'd choose one with either a French or an Indiana blade" (an Indiana blade could be considered a cross between a Colorado and a French blade).

Blade color is extremely important, too, Dick feels. "There seems to be better colors on certain lakes than others. I don't know why that is. I probably fish chartreuse or the "flame" (a chartreuse blade splashed with blaze orange) blade more than any other color, and I also like a copper color in most of the Wisconsin lakes. In Canada, it seems that a red or an orange blade is the top producer, by far."

True, Dick doesn't put much faith in tail color, but there is one rule he follows — to use mixed colors, rather than a single-colored tail. "It's just a little more for the muskies to see. I use solid colors a lot, but I've had better luck on shaded patterns. Contrasting colors just might break up that solid mass of hair and have more appeal to the muskies.

"And when I go fishing, I'll often use the same bucktail all day. The only time I'll change the color of the hair itself is when I'm fishing after dark. Then I'll use a white bucktail so I can see it coming through the water. That's it."

For years, the standard musky bucktail has had a black tail. Dick acknowledges that, but he qualifies it, too. "I really believe there are more fish caught on black bucktails, but it's only because more guys use black bucktails than any other color. If they'd try other colors, especially contrasting colors, their catches would probably increase."

Not only do musky fishermen handicap themselves through extensive and sometimes exclusive use of black bucktails, but they also hamper themselves by using equipment that is simply too heavy, Dick feels. "Everybody gears up like they're going to catch a world record musky. That's just not going to be the case so why not enjoy yourself with the fish you do catch? Why do we handicap ourselves with tackle that would

Dick Moore controls his boat from the bow, easing it onto a be-tween island bar as darkness falls over Lake Tomahawk.

handle a 60-pound fish when we aren't going to hook one any-way," he mused.

He also feels musky anglers use too big of a bucktail. "I have no belief whatsoever in the axiom 'big bait, big fish'," Dick said. "I think the influx of people using huge bucktails started in Canada by musky fishermen who were simply trying to keep northern pike off their bucktails. A big musky will eat a small bucktail, and a small musky will hit a big bucktail. Just use an average size, and you should be all right."

Dick's equipment would be considered light by most musky anglers. He does use a heavy leader, generally a piece of solid wire measuring .041 to .045 inches in diameter with a Berkley Crosslock snap and a ball bearing swivel. That's tied to Gude-brod GT teflon-coated braided dacron line, usually in the 20- to 25-pound test range. Dick's rods are custom made 6-1/2- to

*"I think the influx of people using huge bucktails started in Can-
ada by musky fishermen who were simply trying to keep northern
pike off their bucktails. A big musky will eat a small bucktail, and
a small musky will hit a big bucktail. Just use an average size, and
you should be all right."*

Dick Moore continued to fish with a bucktail despite an approaching cold front, and his patience paid off with the only catch of the day — an undersized musky.

7-1/2-footers, constructed from St. Croix graphite blanks. On top of his rods, he mounts Ambassadeur 7000 baitcasting reels.

Dick believes strongly in a steady retrieve of bucktails, using a fast retrieve only during the hottest days of summer. He feels bucktails will work at any time of year, at any time of day. "I'll throw bucktails from opening day until the lakes freeze," he smiled. "They're just such an effective bait. You can work them fast when the water's warm, and you can work them slow when it's cold. These fish don't read all the fishing magazines that tell you that bucktails shouldn't be used in the

73

A selection of the bucktails tied by Dick Moore, seen in his base-ment shop. From left, are: King Tut, Seducer, Muskie-Teer Cana-dian, Crystal Tail, and Muskie Buzzer.

fall. If they want to eat it, they'll eat it, no matter what time of year it is.

"You just have to remember to slow the bait down in the spring and fall when the water is cold because the musky's metabolism is low and they aren't going to chase a fast-moving bait. If you slow a bucktail down, there's no reason why they shouldn't work all season long."

If there is one secret to retrieving a bucktail, Dick says it's to have the bucktail's blade spinning the moment it hits the water. "I actually start my retrieve before the bucktail hits the water to ensure that the blade is turning. Often, the strike will come as soon as that bait hits, but a lot of bucktails just won't start spinning if you don't start your retrieve right away," he said.

The real key to catching muskies on bucktails is to know where the best spots are on a lake and then use bucktails, Dick insisted. "I have no secrets with my bucktails. Heck, a bucktail's a bucktail. I cast them out and retrieve them. That's it."

Dick Moore no longer guides, but information on his tackle company and fishing products can be obtained by calling him at (715) 356-6834.

Chapter Six

Night Fishing with Joe Bucher

For sheer beauty, there's nothing like a big musky gliding through the water. Graceful movements belie the awesome power contained within those striped sides and the unimaginable terror those dagger teeth must inflict in baitfish.

Illuminated by headlamps worn by Joe Bucher and myself, more than 20 pounds of musky swam alongside Bucher's Ranger boat. A big, thick, healthy fish, this 40-inch-plus whopper was merely catching its wind before yet another line-stripping run. And as the fish walked me around the boat, I was taken aback as I glimpsed a reddish moon easing its way upward from the horizon — the musky had been hooked just when Joe said it would.

Earlier that day, when Joe and I spoke on the telephone about what time we should meet for our musky outing, he said going out before 7:30 wouldn't be worth the effort. "For the past week there's been a 'window' from around 9 o'clock to 10:30 when they're biting," Joe said. "Before or after that they just aren't moving. Last night, we caught six muskies and six walleyes, all within that time frame. And the bigger ones seem to want to bite just when the moon is rising."

As I write this chapter, less than two days after Joe and I fished together, I'm still amazed at how he was able to call the shots that evening. Joe literally knew when the musky would feed before it did. As a friend whom I told the above story to mused, "It's scary when somebody knows so much, isn't it?"

Joe Bucher is considered by many to be the best musky guide in all of Wisconsin, and that's quite a statement considering the other top guides who are included in this book. During his career he's put numbers in the boat, with 211 legal fish one season, and he's caught huge muskies — including one day in Canada when he caught and released two 40-pound-plus fish. Most musky anglers will go a lifetime without even seeing a 40-pounder in the water, much less catching one.

Joe has accomplished much of his success as a tradition breaker. He moved to Boulder Junction, Wisconsin, in 1976 and became a guide, cold turkey, towing a boat that was considered big at the time — a Lund guide boat with swivel seats and a 25-horsepower outboard. Many of the old-time guides and other locals scoffed at this youngster that first year, and as Joe's wife, Beth, described it, "We starved that winter." He charged $50 a day, much more than most guides charged, and promoted himself constantly either by writing in *Fishing Facts* magazine or by driving to Milwaukee to give seminars at the inexpensive rate of $50. And, Joe adds, self-promotion was something you just weren't supposed to do back then.

Today, Joe Bucher, now of Eagle River, is a one-man show. He's got his own line of fishing tackle, his own television fishing show, he's editor of *Musky Hunter* magazine, a field editor of *Fishing Facts,* and represents numerous fishing companies, including top-of-the-line Ranger Boats. Promoting himself

"I'm thinking that we've forced muskies into biting at night because there are certain criteria for what makes a great night fishing lake. Number one, you need heavy boat traffic, and number two, you need somewhat clear water. I sometimes wonder if in the days before big boat traffic there was a need to fish at night."

got Joe Bucher started, but he's stayed at the top because he catches fish.

And he considers night fishing for muskies the single best technique for much of the season. Remember, he's a tradition breaker, and fishing after dark for muskellunge is a major, major change from the status quo.

"When I was younger down in the Milwaukee area, I played for a rock and roll group called 'Raven Strait'," Joe recalled. "When we got done doing a gig, the rest of the guys would go to bed. But I went fishing. I caught lots of bass and walleyes, and found that lakes that received lots of boat traffic yet had relatively clear water had the best night fishing.

"When I started guiding, I fished the usual nine to five shift like all the other guides. It was moderately productive early and late in the year, but during July and August it was a real bust. If you caught a musky a week you were doing well.

"Then, when my tackle business started to take off, I decided to fish early and late in the day and work on baits during the day, leaving those midday hours to the power boats. We started to catch more muskies, but always at the end of the day or sometimes after dark, and I always thought they were a fluke," Joe continued.

"Once I was out all day with some guys in this type of weather (the day I interviewed Joe, Aug. 29, 1991, was 90 degrees-plus and muggy). Nothing happened all day. We got some supper and fished all evening. Nothing. Right at the end of the day we got two fish, boom-boom. So we kept fishing, and we ended up catching eight muskies, still one of the best nights I've ever had. The fish were still biting, but we finally got so tired we just had to go in."

Beth Bucher, who was along for this interview, smiled at Joe. "He started releasing fish before anyone else did, too. He'd come in and say he released a fish, and people wouldn't

Eagle River, Wisconsin, Guide Joe Bucher works to unhook the author's 44-inch musky.

believe him because you just didn't do that back then. Then he started night fishing, and it was ideal. All the people who would follow him around couldn't see what he was doing anymore, and they just couldn't believe the fish he was catching. So he started telling people exactly how he caught them, and they still didn't believe him. Half the fun was fooling those kind of people," she remembered. Of course, "those kind of people" had to be convinced their traditional tactics were not always right.

For years people didn't believe that muskies fed at night because northern pike seldom do. "I think the first mistake there is that we associate muskies too closely with northerns," Bucher said. "These are different creatures. A pike will rarely bite at night, but muskies, in some lakes, may do all of their feeding then.

"I believe that muskies have far better eyesight than northerns. That was driven home to me on a lake up in Canada, which has high clay banks and gets murked up when the wind blows. If the water's clear, you'll catch northerns right along with the muskies. But as soon as the wind blows and it murks up, the pike quit but the muskies keep right on feeding."

That theory is supported by the fact that tiger muskies, which are crossbreeds between northern pike and muskies,

After unhooking the musky, Bucher hefts it to admire it in the glow of his headlamp.

Joe Bucher tilts the author's 44-inch musky sideways to show off its beautiful markings to the camera.

seldom feed during night hours. "We should call them 'tiger pike.' They're much more similar to pike than to muskies," Joe feels.

Bucher wonders if man's use of bigger and more powerful speedboats hasn't forced muskies into an exclusive night-bite in some lakes. "I'm thinking that we've forced them into biting at night because there are certain criteria for what makes a great night fishing lake. Number one, you need heavy boat traffic, and number two you need somewhat clear water. I sometimes wonder if in the days before big boat traffic there was a need to fish at night."

Still, muskies do not have the best of vision under low light, but then few things do. For that reason, Bucher says a good night bait must consist of the "two V's" — visibility and vibra-

Water flies as Joe Bucher sets the hook on a musky that hit at boatside.

tion. "That's what you really need in a lure. Something he can see and something he can find easily. So you need a big bait for the musky to see it, and it has to make noise. That's why jerk baits really aren't a good night bait. They come through the water too easily, and they're too erratic for the fish to find it."

Bucher likes a big, black bucktail with noisy blades, either of a Colorado-type or willow leaf-type blade. "The Colorado has a better thump-thump than the classic fluted blade, and a heavy willow blade is almost as good," he said. Bucher Tackle Co. makes a heavy-bladed willow bucktail for this very reason, called the "Willow Buck." Tandem spin bucktails are also a great bait, he said, and a trick he's learned is to flatten the front blade with a hammer for greater vibration.

Surface baits, when conditions are right, are the classic night lure. "Only certain ones are good night baits," Bucher said. "You need a bait like the Hawg Wobbler, the Creeper or the Jitterbug, something that makes lots of noise with little forward movement, for consistent catches. These types of baits give the musky lots of time to home in on your lure."

What Joe calls THE night bait is a big crankbait, like the "Depth Raider" manufactured by Bucher Tackle Co. "A lot of the field testing that went into the Depth Raider was done at night," Joe said. "It has the profile of a fish going through the water, it's big, and it gives off a great wobble. And the straight model has a bead in it to give off a rattle, which further helps fish locate it."

The Depth Raider is manufactured of a bullet-proof plastic

Joe Bucher's musky goes airborne in an attempt to shake the stinging hooks.

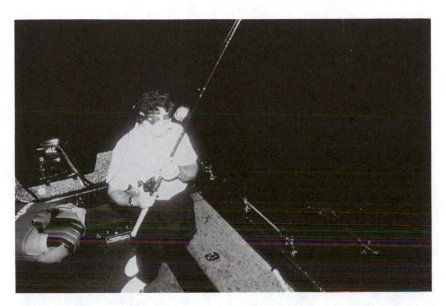

Joe Bucher's musky lies briefly at boatside before resuming its battle.

with a molded-in lip and an extremely buoyant tail section. "Of all the crankbaits out there, the one component missing is durability. I'd get a good crankbait and catch three or four muskies on it and it was bye-bye. The wood baits just didn't hold up. The original Depth Raiders were carved of wood, but when I started to manufacture it I wanted a bait that would work right away and hold up."

To his bait, Joe attaches a 12-inch flexible wire leader of 40- or 50-pound test. That's connected to Magna-Thin copolymer line, again of 40- or 50-pound test. "The heavier line is broader, and that helps keep the bait from diving too deeply into the weeds," he explained. Joe uses heavy-action, seven-foot Gander Mountain rods and Quantum Pro series reels.

Other essentials for night fishing are a headlamp and some

kind of interior boat light, be it a flashlight or whatever. Clean boat layout is a must, and Joe takes only a small selection of lures, two rods, a big landing net, and his unhooking tools with him. All other gear is stowed below deck.

When Joe and I fished together we hit the right conditions for night musky action. The weather had been hot and muggy for a solid week, something Joe feels translates into an extended night bite. And that evening, we fished in golf shirts and shorts, only needing a light jacket when we quit at 1 a.m. "Still, a ten- or 15-minute period after dark may be the only time to catch fish when a big cold front moves through," he added. "You can be on the lake all day without seeing a fish, and as soon as it gets dark you'll hit a fish or two. That's how consistent night fishing is."

Finally spent, Bucher's fish lies at boatside, ready to be unhooked.

Joe Bucher unhooks his musky, which measured 38 inches in length.

During the months of July and August Bucher fishes almost exclusively at night for muskies because of the heavy boat traffic on the Vilas County lakes. Early September, he feels, is the best time to catch a big musky after dark, though he's not sure exactly why this is.

Nobody apparently told the big musky I hooked at the beginning of this chapter it was supposed to wait until September to feed, although it missed by only a little more than two days. Joe and I had been casting Depth Raiders over the deeper weeds of North Twin Lake in Vilas County for 45 minutes when the musky belted my bait about ten feet from the boat and then exploded on the surface as I set the hook.

Water flew in all directions and I frantically worked to get the button pushed on my Ambassadeur 6500C to give the fish line. As soon as I pushed the button the fish ripped off 15 yards of the 30-pound test Berkley line, heading directly away from the boat. Joe already had his headlamp on, and I paused briefly to turn the switch on mine. Slowly I pumped the fish closer to the boat, but with a splash it power dived and charged, running completely under the boat. I plunged the rod tip into the water and walked around the bow. Amazingly, I still had not seen the musky.

On the other side of the boat now, the fish rose to within a foot or two of the surface to where our headlamps picked it up. It was bigger than we initially thought, and its sheer beauty in the clear night water was quite evident. This musky had a broad back and nicely detailed stripes on its sides, certainly the fish we were after.

Again the musky dove, this time swimming around the bow of the boat. It walked me around the Ranger once again, and I tried briefly to lift it near the surface to where Joe had the net. That prompted a quick roll, but the fish only had enough strength remaining to lead me back to the other side of the boat. There Joe expertly slipped the big Beckman net under the fish, and the battle was over.

In the bathtub-sized livewell of the Ranger, the musky measured 44 inches long, and we estimated its weight at 22 or 23 pounds. After a few photos it was released, and with a powerful slap of its tail the musky returned to haunt the lake's depths.

"I was beginning to get a little worried. We didn't hear any baitfish up on the surface yet tonight, and the moon was just starting to rise," Joe said. "You can fish rock humps, sand bars or weed beds, and they all can be good. The key ingredient, however, is baitfish, and if they're up on the surface the

Joe Bucher admires a five-pound walleye that struck a Depth Raider being fished for muskies.

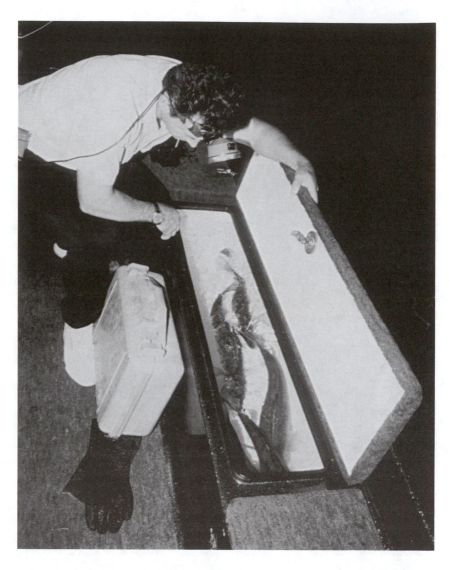

The livewell of Joe Bucher's boat filled up fast with walleyes that, like the muskies, found the Depth Raiders to their liking.

night musky feed should be good."

The moon, Joe explained, is a key ingredient in night musky fishing but not in the way most anglers think. Many feel the bit of light given off by the moon helps muskies see the bait, but Joe disagrees. "There is something to the theory that big muskies feed around a full moon, but not when the moon is up. Even during the day, if a full moon is out the fishing won't be very good. I prefer to fish before the moon rises or just after."

Joe and I resumed fishing after releasing the 44-incher, and the moon theory came through again. Just 12 minutes after easing my fish back in the water, Joe connected while figure-eighting next to the boat. "There's one!" he blurted, setting the hook as water shot ten feet in the air. This fish, which

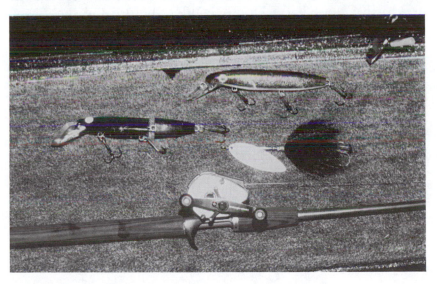

Fishing guide Joe Bucher's favorite night baits include jointed and straight model Bucher Depth Raiders, and a Bucher Willow Buck willow-leaf bladed bucktail.

measured 38 inches, splashed a gallon or two of water into the boat in a short but spirited boatside battle. It, too, was released.

"I recommend doing a full figure eight after every cast because you can't see a follower," Joe explained. "Here it paid off with a nice fish, but the ultimate night experience is to catch a big one on a figure eight at night. The best night of musky fishing I've ever had we boated 11 fish, and the 11th hit on a figure eight. It weighed 35 pounds, eight ounces. What a way to cap off the night!"

Just as fast as the action happened, it was over. The reddish moon was gaining altitude in the eastern sky, and the musky bite simply shut down. Big walleyes, however, apparently aren't affected by the moon, and we caught a half-dozen from two to five pounds on Depth Raiders before the night was over. But that's another story.

"People don't believe me that you can catch these big walleyes at night right along with the muskies on these big baits," Joe said. "But they didn't use to believe me that I was catching big muskies at night, either."

Yes, Joe Bucher has always been a tradition-breaker.

To contact Joe Bucher for a day of fishing or for information about his baits, call him at (715) 479-8849.

Chapter Seven

Trolling with Brian Long

"Here comes a fish. Geez he's a nice one. Oh, he turned off! See the boil?" Brian Long's rapid fire description caused me to turn around just in time to see a bathtub sized swirl about 10 feet from the boat.

"He was coming to eat it, that's for sure," Brian continued, his voice rising with excitement. "That was a reeeaaalll musky."

Then, self-consciously, he smiled. "Did you notice how my voice rose an octave higher when I saw the fish? That's the way you can tell if I just saw a nice musky. My voice gets higher. And that was a nice fish. He was just over 40 inches long and probably about 20 pounds."

Five minutes later Brian spotted another musky swimming quickly toward the boat, following just inches behind his bucktail. This fish, which was about 37 or 38 inches long, also veered off when it got close to the boat.

"That's two nice muskies on top of this bar, and both of them looked mean," Brian said. "But that's the way trolling is. It's either hit or miss. We trolled all afternoon and didn't do anything, and here we do a little casting just before we quit and we see two muskies. Trolling is just another tool, just another piece in the musky fishing puzzle. It sure doesn't rape a lake. We proved that today."

Brian Long, of Glidden in southern Ashland County in extreme northern Wisconsin, is an expert troller for muskies, either power trolling or row trolling. And he's heard all the arguments against trolling, that it's too easy and that it allegedly "rapes a lake."

"Did we rape the lake today? Heck, no. If we'd have been casting we probably would have caught a three-footer. But I don't care if I ever catch a three-footer trolling. I'm not after a three-footer. If I was after a three-footer, we'd have been casting surface baits up against the shoreline," Brian explained. "It actually takes longer to catch a musky trolling than casting because it's a technique for big fish. When I'm trolling, I'm after a monster. When our reels scream, it's not going to be a little one."

Brian and I fished together Friday, Sept. 13, 1991, a humid, overcast day in northwestern Wisconsin. From about 3 p.m. until just before dark, Brian had maneuvered his Tuffy Rampage along the dropoffs and rock bars of Lake Namekagon in southern Bayfield County. Namekagon if one of the few musky lakes in northern Wisconsin where forward motor trolling is a legal technique. Backtrolling, a tactic in which the boat operator runs his boat in reverse, and row trolling are legal throughout Wisconsin.

With three large, slow-wobbling crankbaits being dragged behind the boat, Brian covered several miles of prime big musky water. With one eye on his paper graph depth finder, he kept the boat over deep water, where, we hoped, a giant musky looking for a meal was lurking.

The depth finder marked several big fish suspended over the deep water, and one constant was that all the muskies marked were positioned near schools of baitfish. Yet none of the fish chose to bite, with the exception of a northern pike of about five pounds that Brian quickly unhooked and released.

When it became apparent we weren't going to catch a musky trolling, Brian and I stopped to cast a rock and weed bar that he had discovered while trolling a few years ago that doesn't show on Namekagon's lake map. "It's a great way to see what's on the bottom of the lake, to learn new fishing spots," Brian explained. "That's why trolling is just anther tool, another technique for becoming a better musky fisherman." That rock and weed bar was where we raised the two muskies at the start of this chapter.

Brian is perhaps as knowledgeable a musky troller as there is in Wisconsin. In 1985 he guided Paul Augustyn of Glidden to a 53-inch 40-pound musky caught while trolling on Lake Namekagon, and each year he and his clients catch several 20-pound-plus fish using the technique. And Brian grew up in Vilas County, Wisconsin, a musky-crazed area where, many years ago, row trolling was about the only way to catch a musky. He also was a personal friend of the late Bob Ellis, a Wisconsinite who practiced and perfected row trolling until his death in 1990.

"My family always row trolled because in the old days they just didn't have good enough equipment to cast. So, row trolling was the way they got most of their fish," Brian said. "They'd throw a lure out behind the boat and start rowing around until they caught a fish."

Even with modern equipment, Brian feels trolling has a

With three lines baited with large crankbaits trailing behind the boat, Brian Long maneuvers his boat over the depths of Lake Namekagon.

place in musky fishing. "It just makes sense. Everybody always says the big muskies are out in the deep water, and then they go fish shallow. I'm convinced there are muskies that never go in shallow water. If a big fish is on a weed bar, somebody's going to hook it because, let's face it, they aren't real intelligent creatures. A big fish in deep water isn't going to see that many baits and might die of old age if we don't catch him today.

"Remember, the Lawtons (Art and Ruth) and the Hartmans (Len and Betty) caught all their big fish trolling," Brian said, referring to the two New York musky-catching couples who in the 1950s accounted for a good portion of the 60-

pound muskies ever recorded. In fact, the late Art Lawton holds the world record with a 69-pound 15-ounce fish. "Most of the biggest muskies in the world were caught trolling. It's obvious. There's a reason for it."

Brian explained that trolling is the most efficient way to reach deep water muskies. "You've constantly got the bait down in the fish zone. You can cast for them, but the baits are only in the fish zone a short amount of time. By trolling, you are always dragging the baits through the fish zone, for miles at a time, without taking them out except when you stop to clear weeds off the lines."

Because of the fact a troller is seeking big muskies, hours of riding in a boat can get boring because there can be a long time between catches. "For most guys to do it, they have to believe in it. You can easily go all day without seeing one fish. You aren't seeing follows, and you aren't getting three-footers banging at the baits," Brian said. "Most of my clients prefer to cast because they want the action. But if I go fishing by myself, I'll take my row trolling boat to a big body of water and troll. If I'm going to catch a world's record, that's how I'm going to do it."

Essentially, the tactics used for row trolling and power trolling are the same — the only thing that differs is the style of boat. If he has a choice, Brian prefers row trolling. "I like the aesthetics of it," he smiled. "It's nice and quiet and it's good exercise. In the shallower lakes, however, it may be more effective because the sound of a boat engine may make the muskies more aware.

"Power trolling's big advantage is comfort, plus you can fish in a gale when you might get blown off the lake in a row trolling boat."

The law also figures in his choice of trolling, Brian noted. "In most parts of Wisconsin, if you don't row troll you have to

"If I go fishing by myself, I'll take my row trolling boat to a big body of water and troll. If I'm going to catch a world's record, that's how I'm going to do it."

backtroll, and that's a hellacious way of doing it unless you go with the wind or use splashguards. It's legal to row troll anywhere."

Power trolling is possible in any style of boat, but Brian prefers big, wide, stable deep-Vs. "If you're after big fish, you're likely on big water," he explained. He does prefer tiller steering for better control of the baits. Conversely, a good row trolling boat is long and narrow and has a sleek look, designed to not have a lot of drag in the back of the boat. "A heavier row trolling boat is actually better than a lighter one because you don't get blown around. Mine's a 15-footer that was designed after an old cypress row boat my grandfather used to have at his resort," he said.

Row trolling may become a thing of the past, Brian feels, simply because it's hard to find that style boat anymore — no boat manufacturer is making them. "Get ahold of an old Rhinelander or Thompson wood boat and fiberglass it tight," he urged. "Otherwise, the only boat being made today that has any real possibility is the Coleman Scanoe. You'd have to modify it, but it's feasible."

Whichever boat he uses, Brian will set out three rods — one on each side pointing out 90 degrees from the side of the boat, and one pointing directly off the back of the boat — in good quality rod holders. The baits on the side rods are placed "a cast and a half" behind the boat while the stern rod is set about 10 yards back from the boat. Brian uses 6-1/2-foot or 7-foot St. Croix Premier musky rods, with Garcia Ambassadeur 6500C reels attached. He's a strong believer in Cortland Muskie Master line in 36-pound test, though when he's fishing deep, clear lakes he may switch to DuPont 14/40 cofilament line. He's also starting to experiment with wire lines for increased depth.

Between the line and the bait Brian attaches a two-foot

long, 90-pound test wire leader. And the bait, he says, will be "the biggest I can get my hands on. I'm trolling for the biggest musky in the lake, and they can eat some pretty big fish."

Brian sets the drags on his reels quite loosely, since the rod is already at a 90-degree angle. A tight drag may result in a broken line or a lost fish because of the heavy pressure exerted by a musky pulling against a moving boat. A line-out clicker on the Ambassadeur reels is engaged to immediately signal a strike, and when the strike does come some trollers will "goose" the engine to set the hook, but not Brian. "I think the motion of the boat has already set the hook. Still, I let 'em have it and set the hook anyway after I take the rod out of the holder. It's in my blood to set that hook."

For really big muskies, Brian prefers a slow troll with baits such as Grandmas, Believers, Bucher Depth Raiders and Rizzo Divers. If he feels a quicker speed is needed to trigger strikes, he'll go to a Bagley Bang-O-B or a Cisco Kid. Lure color varies with the lake.

"Both clear and dark water lakes have their advantages for trolling," Brian said. "Dark water...the lakes themselves are shallower, so there's not as much water to strain. But you have to put your bait closer to the fish for them to find it, and you've got to use a bright bait, and I prefer some kind of fluorescent color.

"In clear water the muskies can see the lure from farther away, but the lakes are typically going to be deeper and the muskies might be at any depth. In these lakes, it's best to use more of a natural colored bait."

Brian will troll in an S-pattern, which varies the speed of the outside lures, often a definite trigger for strikes. For example, when he turns to the left, the bait on the right side of the boat speeds up while the bait on the port side slows or pauses. When turning to the right, its vice versa.

The best place to troll for big muskies, Brian feels, is what he calls the "second dropoff." Just what is the second dropoff? "It's a very hard place to cast to, but it's the second edge before the lake bottom gives way to the lake basin. Fish naturally relate to this, both baitfish and predators, like muskies. And watch the thermocline on your depth finder. Usually, fish will be lying where the thermocline meets the second dropoff, lying in that cooler water.

"To be a good troller, you really have to know a lake well. Otherwise, your baits are constantly running into shallower water and getting hung up."

The second dropoff is a good rule of thumb in darker water lakes, such as Lake Namekagon, where the muskies predominantly feed on suckers and walleyes. In clear water lakes that have ciscos and whitefish, which really don't relate to any structure but tend to hang out in open water, muskies will follow these baitfish and could be anywhere in the lake. Finding baitfish is critical for trollers, and that's why Brian uses a Lowrance X-16 paper graph depth finder. "If it's down there, it'll show on the paper," Brian said.

Brian doesn't believe it's critical for a lure to get very deep, just down 10 to 15 feet. "Bob Ellis told me he used to weight his baits so they went right down to the bottom, and sometimes to whatever level he felt the muskies were at. Bob was convinced after all the years he fished it was better to have the bait unweighted. His baits ran 15 to 20 feet deep and he would fish them over 100 feet of water. He believed that the most active muskies, the ones most likely to bite, were higher in the water."

Weather conditions and time of day don't make much difference to the troller, though Brian prefers calm days when row trolling ("You don't have to work so hard"). If there is a better time to be trolling, Brian likes the evening hours. As for time of year, trolling is best in fall, Brian believes, because the "big fish are just feeding more aggressively." Still, one of the biggest muskies Brian has hooked while trolling struck in summer, actually just about a month before he and I fished together.

"I was row trolling when all of a sudden the boat just stopped. I mean, it just stopped. I thought, 'What's going on?' and then this big musky just came up to the surface and shook its head," Brian said, his voice characteristically rising an octave. "It just had a monstrous head, and it just wallowed and shook back and forth. I could see the bait the whole time swinging back and forth in its mouth, so it must have just been hooked with the tail hook. Anyway, before I could grab the

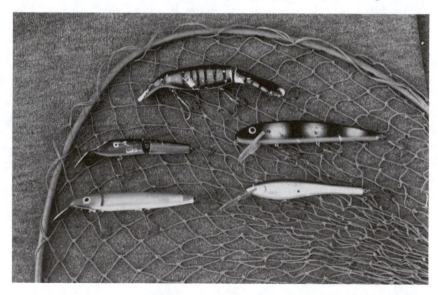

Some of Brian Long's favorite trolling baits. Top row — Believer; second row — Rizzo Diver, Grandma; third row — Cisco Kid, Bagley Bang-O-B.

rod to fight the fish it threw the bait. I couldn't believe it...that fish stopped my boat."

There is a safety factor involved in trolling Brian cautioned about. "You've always got to deal with other boats crossing behind your lines when you're trolling, but when row trolling it's just horrible. Row trolling is still a novelty, and people will motor over close to see what you're doing. You've got to constantly be aware of what other boats are doing.

"I used to wear a dark colored jacket when I row trolled so I wouldn't stand out. But since Bob Ellis got killed (he died in a boating accident in which his row boat was struck by a power boat) I've been wearing a bright red jacket anytime I go out."

In many areas, especially in Wisconsin, power trolling carries a stigma about it. Even the National Fresh Water Fishing Hall of Fame in Hayward, Wisconsin, recognizes two different record categories for muskies — conventional angling and power trolling. Still, whether the effort be by outboard or by oar, trolling is an effective method for catching big muskies and for learning new places to fish.

"Otherwise, I wouldn't do it," Brian smiled.

To contact Brian Long for a day of fishing, call him at (715) 264-4974.

Chapter Eight

Jerk Baits with Dave Dorazio

When Dave Dorazio guides someone on Sawyer County, Wisconsin's sprawling Chippewa Flowage, he prefers to keep his options open. And that's why we were switching tactics.

Dorazio, who manufactures the famous Eddie Bait, a gliding type jerk bait, wanted to show me everything he knows about fishing that type of musky bait. But the day we fished together, Sunday, Sept. 22, 1991, a strong wind gusted from the southwest and lathered the surface of the Big Chip. That same wind kept Dorazio's boat drifting so quickly it was virtually impossible to fish a jerk bait properly.

"We just can't keep up with them," he explained. "We're not imparting any action to the bait...all we're doing is retrieving line and not really doing anything with the bait itself."

Sure, we had tried the lee side of islands and points to get out of the wind. There, Dave produced a jerk bait wizardry that few can match. It's just that the muskies weren't responsive in the slack water areas.

"As long as we know they're going to ignore our jerk baits in the shallows, let's go see if they'll ignore some crankbaits out in the depths," Dave quipped.

He motored the big Tuffy boat into one of the natural lakes that was flooded when the Chippewa Flowage was created in the early years of the 20th century. On this particular lake (which shall remain nameless should its mention pinpoint a pair of big muskies), a friend of Dave's had lost a musky the day before that he estimated to be about 52 inches long. And Dave knew of a 50- incher that hung out there, too.

In a trough between two weed flats, Dave stopped the boat and we each snapped on diving crankbaits — Dave a Cisco Kid and myself a Bucher Depth Raider. Halfway through the first drift a musky followed my straight model Depth Raider

Dave Dorazio at the helm of his Tuffy Marauder during an un-usually windy day on the Chippewa Flowage.

to boatside, though it arrived after I had made a retrieve-ending figure-eight and my next cast had already been launched. Dave got a brief glimpse of the fish as it veered off; my eyes were already watching my next cast.

"There's a good fish," he called out. "I'm not saying it was a 40-pounder, but it was no 40-incher."

On the next drift Dave had a follow from a fish he judged to be in the 20-pound class, and then I had a follow from a fast-moving 20-pounder that actually brushed the Depth Raider with a closed mouth. I was stunned that the chunky musky hadn't taken the bait as it spun around and headed back for the depths.

Though that was the extent of our musky action on that particular day, Dave proved his worth as a guide by changing tactics when the preferred method — jerk baits — wasn't working. He certainly put me onto some nice fish, and he later proved his knowledge of jerk baits during the day-long interview.

"I'm not like some guys who might say 'All I use is Eddie Baits.' I don't. I have no idea how some guys can limit themselves to a jerk bait...to a surface bait, or to a bucktail. When I'm guiding, I tell people to never limit themselves. If your technique isn't working, do something different until you catch fish," Dave explained.

Dave was born and raised on the Chippewa Flowage as his parents owned the Arrow Resort on the Chip's west side. He's been a fishing guide all his life, starting as a teenager taking resort guests out for pocket change. He prefers to fish and guide for muskies, and as he puts it, "catching walleyes is like kissing your sister."

Watching Dave maneuver his Tuffy Marauder among the stumps and bogs of the Chip you can tell he knows it as well as his backyard, and possibly even better. Then when he works

106

an Eddie Bait, you can easily see that he's a master of the jerk bait. He should be, after all, since he handles each and every Eddie Bait that leaves his shop.

Dave has heard all the jokes about jerk baits being named for the fisherman casting them. While he can smile at the jokes, he's very serious about how effective a jerk bait can be for muskies. After all, making baits that catch muskies, and helping clients catch muskies, is his business.

Already an accomplished fishing guide in the early 1980s, Dave admits he needed something to do in the winter when the musky season closed and the lakes froze. A guiding client of his wanted desperately to get into the tackle business, so together they pursued the purchase of an established tackle company. Eddie Ostling, the creator of the Eddie Bait, was interested in selling, and in 1984 the deal became official. "We were very interested in the Eddie Bait when we found out it was for sale," Dave explained. "When you think of musky fishing you think of jerk baits. You think of Eddies, Suicks, Bobbies, the standards. We had an opportunity for one of those baits, so we jumped at it."

Wisconsin's Chippewa Indians are credited by lure historians with making the first jerk baits, either affixing them with hooks or using them as decoys to lure muskies close enough to a canoe to spear. Jerk baits have lived on with sport anglers for a simple reason — they catch muskies.

"A jerk bait either appears as a wounded fish or a feeding fish to muskies. Of course, a wounded baitfish is an easy meal, so a musky will pounce on it," Dave said. "But a feeding fish is also an easy meal. It may be a perch darting through a school of minnows or insect larvae and feeding and not paying attention to what's around it. Again, the musky sees it as an easy meal.

"But also jerk baits are usually so erratic. A musky will fol-

Fishing the lee side of an island, Dave Dorazio retrieves an Eddie Bait toward his boat.

low one out of curiosity when suddenly it takes a turn the musky didn't expect and he hits it out of reflex action."

For these reasons jerk baits are deadly for muskies in all types of water — clear or stained, deep or shallow. "I really don't know of a lake they won't work in," Dave reasoned. "But there are lakes where they do work better than in others. They work great in some dark water lakes and not so well in others, and work well in some clear water lakes and not so well in other clear lakes. It just depends on the lake."

Essentially, a jerk bait is a slab of wood measuring from about six inches in length up to a foot or more. Various cuts in the wood or bendable fins attached create drag when the bait moves through water, and it is retrieved with short jerks or pulls on the line to impart a diving, darting action.

There are three types of jerk baits, although one type could probably be considered a hybrid. There are gliders, like the Eddie or the big Reef Hawg, which have a pronounced side-to-side glide as their primary action; choppers, like the Suick or the Bobbie, which dive when pulled and then rise on the pause in a pull-stop-pull retrieve pattern; and the "hybrids," or big crankbaits that twitch as they are retrieved in the same pull-stop-pull manner. Baits in this category would be Grand-mas, Crane Baits or Rapalas. Of course, this is far from a complete list of all brands of gliders, choppers and hybrids, but these popular plugs are merely being listed as examples.

Dave feels that there is no single jerk bait or jerk bait type that is better than others as they vary by application. Of course, the Eddie is his favorite, but he admits to carrying Suicks and Bobbies in his tackle box. "I've caught a lot of fish on Suicks and Bobbies. If you want to fish over the tops of weeds or in pockets in the weeds, then a Suick or a Bobbie is a great bait. And there are times when muskies simply prefer to hit a bait that stops and rises. I don't know why they are that way sometimes, but you'd be a fool not to throw a chopper when the muskies want them."

Gliders have their own applications, too, Dave explained. "A small Eddie Bait (the six-inch model) is perfect for working over the tops of weeds. Sometimes a fish just wants that bait gliding back and forth over the weeds. And the big Eddie (the eight-inch model) is a good bait occasionally in spring, but it really comes into its own in the fall when the water cools to the low 50s or even the 40s. You pull the Eddie and it glides to the side and just hangs there, and some of them hang forever. And that's when they're going to get eaten."

Hybrids, or twitch baits, are effective because their wide sizes give off flash to fish below. Dave particularly likes the Grandma for its wide wobble and flat sides.

When we fished together Dave and I threw all three types of jerk baits but couldn't entice a muskellunge into striking any of them. His retrieve pattern with a small Eddie seemed to be a rapid side-to-side twitch, and the bait performed magically as if it had a mind of its own.

"That's the beauty of jerk baits. They really have no action except what you put into them," Dave smiled. "The yanks and twitches you impart with your rod tip will make the bait dive or swing to the side, or sometimes pop completely out of the water. It's all up to you and what you do with the rod." He keeps his rod tip low to the water as he makes short, quick pulls, all the while retrieving slack line. Another advantage to holding the rod in this manner is it allows for a wide, sweeping hookset. "Most jerk baits are a big chunk of wood that a musky, especially a big one, can get a good grip on. If you don't move the bait in the fish's mouth, you'll never hook it," Dave noted.

Since jerk baits are made of wood they vary considerably even within the same brand, and Dave recommends an angler

Chippewa Flowage guide Dave Dorazio keeps his boat positioned near one of the Chip's many bogs as he searches for muskies.

practice until he becomes proficient with certain baits and knows how they will perform. "A guy might have 12 Eddie Baits in his tackle box, but he'll have two or three that work just a little different from the others, or he can make them do something the others won't do. You wouldn't be able to get him to trade one of those baits for a rod, a boat or a truck. They have learned how to use those particular baits, and they have confidence in them. And confidence in a bait makes you throw it that much more, and eventually work it that much better," Dave said.

For better control of a jerk bait, Dave recommends anglers

use non-stretch braided dacron ("I hate using rubber line," he says about monofilament). Dave uses 30-pound test Cortland Micron, eventually switching to 40-pound test in the fall when he's casting big Eddies. For a leader, all Eddies come equipped with a wire leader of stiff .035-inch diameter, and Dave affixes a number eight split ring in the nose of his own baits for a wider side-to-side glide.

When casting smaller jerk baits like small Eddies, Dave prefers a seven-foot St. Croix rod for better twitching control. With larger baits, he goes to the six-foot St. Croix or the six-foot nine-inch model. "A stiff rod is probably more important with jerk baits than with surface baits or bucktails because you are the one giving the bait action. The movements you make with the rod will then be duplicated by the bait," Dave said.

For reels, Dave uses the Ambassadeur 5500C because he palms the reel and its smaller size fits better in his hand. He said he's tried others, and has yet to find one that works as well while taking the abuse of casting heavy jerk baits.

Since jerk baits are so "personal," meaning they have no other action than what the angler creates, the matters of color and modifications vary from angler to angler. "Color is basically a matter of personal preference," Dave feels. "But that's the same with any kind of bait. But the rule to follow, if there is such a thing, is light color baits in clear lakes, and dark or fluorescent color baits in dark water. But that doesn't mean that a dark bait won't work in clear water, and that a light-colored bait won't work in dark water."

The one key to getting a musky to bite a jerk bait, Dave said, is what he calls the "roll," or when a jerk bait rolls onto its side during a retrieve before settling into a normal position. "A color change makes a difference. If a musky is looking up at a wounded baitfish and is seeing its belly but suddenly it sees the darkness of its sides, that's a triggering effect. Maybe it shows weakness in the baitfish. And a jerk bait has to have that sudden color change, or 'roll,' to be effective," Dave explained. "That's why you won't see me throwing a jerk bait that is a solid color. Sure, I make them because I sell a bunch. Somebody is catching fish with them. But I want some kind of color contrast, to better show off that roll to a following musky."

Dave recommends that an angler buying a jerk bait first check that all screw eyes and hook hangers are in a straight axis along the bait's body. "If they aren't in a straight line, that bait just isn't going to work well," he explained. "Even the slightest thing out of whack will cause the bait to move differently through the water."

Just as retrieve technique and color preference varies from angler to angler, so do modifications. Since most jerk baits are constructed of wood, just about anything can be done to modify their action.

Some anglers weight their jerk baits in an attempt to achieve neutral buoyancy, or as Dave puts it, "increase the hang time." The theory behind this is a slower rising jerk bait appears more lifelike to a following musky, making the predator more inclined to strike. Dave suggests that an angler drill a hole in the bait he's planning to weight just behind the front hook, which is usually the balancing point. An egg sinker can be tapped into the hole, or it can be filled with molten lead. Since gliders like the Eddie usually are already weighted, Dave and other anglers scratch the paint off the lead and the surrounding wood and then store their baits in the livewells of their boats when not in use. The baits then soak up water and gain additional weight.

Some fishermen add spinner blades to a bait's tail for additional flash, and many will change the hook arrangement or cut off the factory hooks and install new ones, attaching them with split rings. The theory behind using split rings is they give a big musky less torque to twist a jerk bait out of its mouth, and they are supposed to somewhat neutralize the force of a musky shaking the heavy jerk baits when they jump. Dave doesn't subscribe to this theory. "I don't put split rings on Eddie Baits when I make them because I don't seem to lose many fish without them," Dave said. "With split rings, I tend to get more tangled hooks, and hooks that come around and hook the bait's body, thus ruining a cast. I'm pretty happy with my hooking percentage without split rings."

Another popular modification is to attach a hook to the back of jerk baits to catch those fish that strike a jerk bait in the back when it rolls. If the hook isn't added, the musky is grabbing the plug on the opposite side of the belly and tail

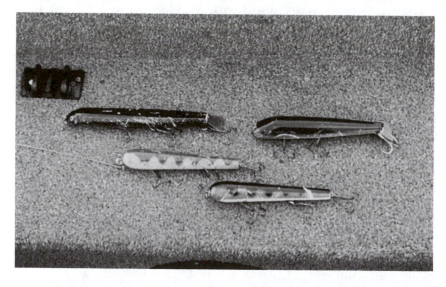

A selection of Dave Dorazio's favorite jerk baits. At top left is a Suick Musky Thriller, and top right is a Bobbie Bait. The other two pictured are Eddie Baits.

hooks and usually doesn't get hooked.

Dave admitted there is plenty that can be done by individual anglers to modify jerk baits. "The best thing an angler can do is experiment and see what he likes best. If it looks good to you in the water, chances are it looks good to the muskies, too. Sooner or later, that bait is going to work for you."

Though the Eddie Bait didn't work the day Dave and I got together, it really didn't have much of a chance to strut its stuff because of the strong wind. But Dave rests his reputation and his livelihood on the big baits working most of the time, so that should tell you something.

To contact Dave Dorazio for a day of fishing, or about Eddie Baits, call him at (715) 462-3885.

Chapter Nine

Vertical Jigging with Bruce Shumway

CLICK!...click...click...click. Like a scene from the movie "Jaws," fishing line started to pay out slowly from the heavy duty fishing rod in the center of the boat. Guide Bruce Shumway and I looked at each other momentarily, and then went into action.

Bruce quickly stepped forward and grabbed the rod, which had continued to slowly give out line. I reeled the heavy bait I had been vertically jigging out of the water, and stowed the rod.

"What's up?" I queried Bruce as he lifted the rod gently, trying to determine what was pulling line from the reel. He smiled, and replied, "We've got one nibbling."

"Nibbling" was an understatement. The rod that was slowly giving line had been baited with a 20-inch long sucker, a large "minnow" that probably weighed somewhere around three pounds. Weighted heavily so it would go to the bottom in the

20-plus-foot depths we were fishing, the sucker had done its job — and had been grabbed by a musky.

"What do you want me to do?" I asked Bruce. I've caught many muskies on suckers, but in this case he was the guide. In his boat, what he says goes. "You take the rod. It's your fish," he smiled, handing the heavy pole to me. I like those kind of directions.

Bruce and I were fishing Middle Eau Claire Lake in southern Bayfield County, Wisconsin, a lake that is part of a chain known to produce some awfully large muskies. In fact, the "unofficial" world record of 70 pounds was caught from the Eau Claire Chain back in 1954. While there was virtually no chance of a record fish on the line this time, the fact that whatever was down there grabbed a 20-inch sucker certainly bode well for a chance at a trophy.

The day was Oct. 20, 1991, and a warming south wind was blowing across the water. Indeed, it was warming, as the temperature was about 35 degrees. The day before, fishermen in the Hayward area woke up to 15-degree temperatures and braved snow squalls that turned the countryside white. Bruce and I didn't fish together that day, but he had guided a client who lost a fish Bruce estimated to be in the 30-pound class. And I had fished by myself, catching and releasing a 15-pound musky and losing a 20-plus pounder. The "sucker bite" was on, and we hoped to boat a whopper to help illustrate this chapter.

Bruce Shumway was chosen to be interviewed because he is pioneering a technique called vertical jigging — in which an angler jigs a heavy bait in an up-and-down manner over deep water. The jig may be struck by a musky, or it may attract a musky that will end up grabbing a sucker. And that's exactly what had happened. As Bruce and I talked about his technique, I had slowly jigged a large, weighted bait called the

Bruce Shumway mans the oars to keep his boat positioned over a musky that grabbed a sucker.

"Fuzzy Duzzit," which happens to be manufactured by Bruce's brother, Hayward guide Bill "Fuzzy" Shumway. I had felt a "tick" on the line as I jigged, but failed to connect when I snapped the rod tip upward to set the hook. Seconds later, the clicker on the sucker rod signalled a bite.

Bruce was on the oars now, trying to keep his big Tuffy Esox Ltd. close to the fish as it ate the sucker. My job was to handle the rod, taking up slack when necessary and trying to determine just what the musky was doing. I switched the rod from hand to hand constantly, plunging the free hand into the pockets of my jacket in an attempt to keep it warm. The musky took its good natured time, as fish that are on the top of a lake's food chain tend to do.

"How long has it been?" I asked Bruce, wiggling the fingers of my right hand in an attempt to regain feeling.

"About ten minutes," Bruce answered, checking his watch. "Watch for him to take off on a run. He'll keep chewing on that big 'sausage' until he's ready to swallow it, and when he does the big head of that sucker will bump him in the back of the throat. That will get him nervous and he'll take off on a run. When he does, engage the forward drive of that reel and set the hook hard."

By the tone of his voice, I could tell Bruce was excited. He liked the fact that the musky had been deep — 26 feet — when it grabbed the sucker. "Little muskies usually don't eat such big suckers. When you use suckers this big, you tend to have action from only the bigger fish," Bruce pointed out. "And, did you notice how he just stopped it and the line paid out slowly, like he owned the lake?"

His excitement was infectious. I had never taken a 30-pound musky, though I've boated fish in the high 20-pound range and have lost 30-pounders. I told this to Bruce. "If we get this fish, and it's a 30, thump it," I said. "I want a 30 for the wall. If this is a 30, we're going to have a party. On me."

Bruce chuckled. "My brother and I were fishing last year on one of the lakes around here and I watched a big musky, that I figured was over 35 pounds, come up and eat the sucker. I handed the rod to Fuzzy because he hasn't caught a fish that big. Pretty soon it started on a run and he set the hook, and everything went right until he got that fish to within about three feet under the boat. He just couldn't get it any closer to the boat to where I could take a stab at it with the net. That musky just kept thrashing and thrashing down there, and pretty soon it ripped the hooks out and swam away.

"Fuzzy just sat down and of course it was pretty quiet for about five minutes. Then he looked at me and said, 'You know, I had visions of drinking whiskey straight from the bottle.'"

When I quit laughing, I checked the musky by slowly lifting the rod upward. A sharp tug indicated he was still there. "How long?" I asked Bruce.

"Twenty minutes. He could have it swallowed any time now, or it could take an hour. Be awake."

As I tended to the musky, Bruce quickly started to prepare his boat. I heard the whir of the power trim tilting the 50-horsepower Mariner out of the water. Then the Minn Kota trolling motor was tilted up, and his big Beckman musky net was readied. Finally, out came the unhooking tools. The serious, business-like manner that Bruce used to ready his boat indicated he also felt we may be dealing with a special fish. My heart pounded.

"How long?"

"Twenty-five minutes."

Bruce continued to work the oars, keeping the boat positioned over the musky. Every couple of minutes I lifted the rod tip to see what the fish was up to. Occasionally, it took a few feet of line in a slow, deliberate manner. For the most part, however, it just lay in the deep water, chewing on the sucker as indicated by the line's heavy twitching.

Bruce looked over his shoulder. "We're getting kind of close to that rock bar. Why's he coming up into shallower water? Damn. The boat's only in 14 feet of water. Check the fish."

I had just checked the fish maybe a minute earlier but followed Bruce's instructions anyway. After all, in his career as a guide he's accounted for well over a dozen muskies surpassing the 30-pound barrier, considered the measure of a true trophy musky. This fish wasn't acting like a big one anymore.

Gradually I eased in line. And more line. Finally, it became apparent the musky had dropped the sucker. I reeled in the big baitfish and found it still lively, with scratches on its sides only about four inches wide. "It's really too hard to estimate how big he was by the bite," Bruce said. "But that one just couldn't handle that big of a sucker, so he couldn't have been too big."

Vertical jigging had almost paid off. While we had spent

Guide Bruce Shumway works a Fuzzy Duzzit in a lift-drop pattern. Muskies will either hit the Fuzzy Duzzit or be attracted to one of the suckers he will have baited on other rods.

over a half-hour waiting in vain for a musky to eat a sucker, chances are the jigging I had been doing had attracted the musky to the area.

"Vertical jigging is just another tool for fishing deep at this time of year, after the turnover," Bruce explained. "If the musky doesn't come over and eat the jigged bait, it may also serve as an attractor to bring the fish within view of the suckers. I definitely feel I get more hits on my suckers when someone is jigging a Fuzzy Duzzit, especially when we're fishing in extremely deep water, over 25 feet. It gets pretty dark down there, even in clear lakes, and the vibrations and flash these baits put out help the muskies find the suckers."

The Fuzzy Duzzit resembles an outsized Sonar, a popular walleye jigging bait. It weighs just short of two ounces and measures a full six inches in length. "Bill was making these for walleyes. I had noticed that occasionally a musky would grab a sucker when I sort of jigged it, so I got the idea of using the Fuzzy Duzzit for muskies.

"The first day out I took my wife Lynn along and told her to jig one of them while I put down the suckers. All of a sudden she asked me if we were in deep water, and I said yes. 'Well, then I've got one,' she said, and she brought up a 36- or 37-inch musky. The next four days I was guiding, and I had one of my clients jig them every day. We caught a fish every one of those days on the Fuzzy Duzzits, including one 26-pounder that had just dropped a sucker. My client was mad about that musky dropping the bait and lowered the Fuzzy Duzzit down there, made two lifts and pow! The fish just inhaled it," Bruce related.

Years ago, Bruce Shumway was known as a "summer slop" fisherman, hitting shallow weeds with a marabou-tailed spinner of his own design, the Bootail. And he took big fish, including his best, a 53-inch 40-pounder in 1985 from Bayfield

County's Lake Namekagon, in just such a manner. And one day he had two 30-pounders in the boat within an hour fishing shallow with Bootails. He's still a great "slop" fisherman, but lately he's become known for his fall musky expertise, and the Fuzzy Duzzit has been one of the keys to that success.

"You know me. In the summer I might fish 30 spots in the course of a day's time. I like fishing shallow and I do well at it. I've always believed that the fisherman who hits the most good spots in a day's time is going to make contact with the most active fish," Bruce said. "But after the turnover, the muskies can be anywhere because they're not kept out of the deeper water by the thermocline. And it just seems the larger muskies are in 20 feet of water or more. It's like fishing two different lakes after the turnover. Before it, you fish shallow, after that, you go deep. I might only fish three or four spots in a day's time in the fall, but I will be over deep water.

"And vertical jigging is the best way to reach deep water fish, with the exception of live bait. Quite often, in late fall, you might be fishing water that's 50 or 55 feet deep. You can't get a crankbait down there. You need a heavy bait that will sink quickly, and the only way to keep it in deep water is to jig it."

Still, vertical jigging is not a fall-only tactic. "I've got good reports from people jigging them right off the deep weedlines in 15 to 18 feet of water," Bruce said. "You can also work them right on the edges of bogs, or along the sides or on top of fish cribs. You have absolute control with a vertical jigging bait, something you can't achieve with any other type of lure."

Bruce fishes the Fuzzy Duzzit with a lift-drop technique, first letting the bait fall to the bottom and then tightening the line so the bait is still on the bottom while the rod tip is touching the water's surface. "You only have to lift it a foot or a foot and a half and then let it drop back to the bottom. And just keep repeating that, although you may have to let out more line or pull some in as the depth changes. It's great for clients because they can keep their mitts on when it's cold and I can tell at a glance if they're working it right. The vibrations the bait puts off translates right up into the rod tip."

You can't miss a musky's strike on a Fuzzy Duzzit, Bruce told me, because they will hit the bait hard. I found this out for myself a week later while fishing over a 30-foot hole in a lake of the Eagle River Chain, in Wisconsin's Vilas County. A musky chose to hit my Fuzzy Duzzit rather than either of the two suckers I had also placed in the depths, and the heavy strike was sensational. I'd like to say I caught the fish, which measured somewhere around 41 or 42 inches long, but it spit the bait in a final leap near the boat after a lengthy battle.

While the Fuzzy Duzzit is his primary jigging presentation, Bruce is also starting to experiment with heavy leadhead jigs of two or three ounces, hooked through the lips of a 10- to 15-inch long sucker and rigged with a "stinger" treble hook in the sucker's back. "A guy I know started using this last fall in flowages because he wanted to get maximum control of his bait for fishing old river beds," Bruce said. "You know, he stuck a couple of 30-pounders doing just that."

For vertical jigging, Bruce uses a seven-foot St. Croix graphite rod with a 5000 series Garcia Ambassadeur reel. It's wound with 20-pound test monofilament line, which allows the bait to drop more quickly than a heavier, thicker, more water-resistant line.

His sucker rods are made of solid fiberglass by St. Croix and have Penn 209 trolling reels and 40-pound Trilene Big Game line attached. "I like the fiberglass because you can really set the hook hard on a musky and not worry about the rod breaking," Bruce explained. "Plus, we're dealing with the biggest fish in the lake, so I prefer to go with heavy equipment."

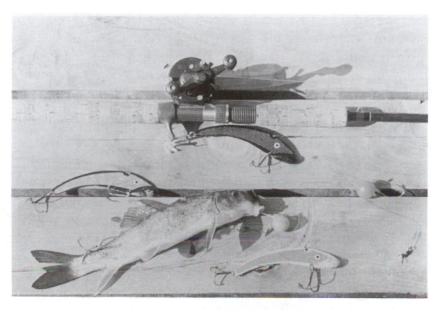

The tools of Bruce Shumway's trade — gold, silver and chartreuse Fuzzy Duzzits encircle a sucker rigged with a heavy two-ounce jig and a stinger hook. A red three-ounce jig is also pictured.

Color preference for Fuzzy Duzzits and other jigging baits varies with the lake, Bruce noted. Lakes that contain ciscoes are perfect for a silver-sided Fuzzy Duzzit, because the artificial bait matches both the color and the size of the baitfish. Where small walleyes are a primary forage, a gold-sided Fuzzy Duzzit works great (Bruce tips the tail hook of a gold Fuzzy Duzzit with a piece of white pork rind to give the illusion of the white tip of a walleye's tail). And in dark water, easily-seen fluorescent colors work better.

In the clear water of the Eau Claire Lake Chain, Bruce had me jigging a silver Fuzzy Duzzit. "That bait really flashes in clear water. The first year I used them, all I had were silver ones, and they worked all over," Bruce said.

Bruce and I didn't have any more action after the heart-thumping excitement of waiting for the musky at the beginning of this chapter to eat the sucker. But the musky apparently did make a grab at the Fuzzy Duzzit before nailing the sucker, as evidenced by the tick I felt on the line, and that certainly indicated the technique works.

Later that day, after Bruce and I had parted company, I spoke with a Wisconsin Department of Natural Resources fisheries clerk who was busy conducting a creel census on the Eau Claire Lakes. He said our near-miss was the only musky action reported by any of the anglers he talked to that day.

If that isn't proof of the effectiveness of vertical jigging in late fall, I don't know what is.

To contact Bruce Shumway about a day of fishing, or about his baits, call him at (715) 798-3441.

Chapter Ten

Crankbaits with Peter Haupt

Only madmen would be out fishing on a day like this, the thought flashed through my mind. Then I corrected myself — madmen and Peter Haupt.

The day — Nov. 11, 1991 — was actually a break from the awful weather Wisconsin had suffered through the first part of the month. November opened with rain, then turned to bone-chilling cold. Over 40 inches of snow was dumped in some places of northwestern Wisconsin, and most of the state's lakes were frozen over. Heck, the two days before I fished with Pete I had watched ice fishermen venture onto Lake Iola, just a short distance from my home.

And Iola is a four-hour drive south of Hayward.

One cannot fault Peter Haupt for going fishing under such conditions. He's a master of the crankbait, and he prefers to fish all the way until ice-up. A mounted, 47-pound musky caught by Pete that now hangs in his Hayward-area restaurant, The Ranch, is testimony to his success. And he's got this mission, a quest if you will, that was given him by onetime Wisconsin Governor Tony Earl, when Earl viewed the 47-pounder.

"He told me to 'catch a bigger fish.' That's what I'm trying to do," the Hayward guide grins when he recalls the day he met the governor. So I reasoned that day, since I'm out here with Pete I must be the madman.

Half of Big Round Lake, which is located northeast of Hayward, Wisconsin, was covered with ice, but what Pete called "the good half" was still open. I'm not sure why it was "the good half," except maybe it was because it still had open water. That open water was not to last long, however, as it was literally freezing around us as we fished. Water near shore was of a gelatinous nature, and we were forced to dip our rods into the lake about every third cast to clear ice from the guides.

"This is trophy musky fishing!" Pete shouted, to no one in particular. I had to agree. We were certainly paying our dues, and if we were going to catch a fish, I figured, it had better be a damn good one.

Keeping one eye on his depthfinder, Pete continually positioned his Alumacraft deep-V near the multitude of humps and bars that Big Round is known for. The only way to describe some of his hot spots is to call them spires. One moment, the boat is over 50 feet of water, and suddenly it's over 10. Then, just as suddenly, the bottom plunges to 60 feet. We cast giant, deep-diving crankbaits over and around these humps, hoping a musky with a big appetite was lurking nearby.

Time after time I watched behind my crankbait as it slowly climbed from the depths, hoping to spot a musky following.

Hayward guide Peter Haupt steers his Alumacraft deep-V over the waters of Big Round Lake in Sawyer County, Wisconsin.

When Pete moved to his favorite hump, which he affection-ately calls the Penny Bar ("It's not on the lake map, but if it was it would be about the size and the shape of a penny"), my attention was at its highest. It was from the Penny Bar that Pete took the 47-pounder, and where he once had a follow from a tiger musky that he figured was in the 55-pound class. A tiger musky, which is a cross between muskellunge and northern pike, rarely will reach 30 pounds, much less 50.

It's an understatement to say Pete wants that fish. After all, that particular tiger musky is bigger than his 47-pounder. It's incentive like that that keeps him going when most fishermen have long before put their boats in storage for the winter.

For as hard as we fished and as stiff as our fingers froze, nothing happened during our afternoon of fishing. Sure, there were instances when our crankbaits dove especially deep on a retrieve and stopped after hitting a rock, thereby causing a brief rush of adrenalin as we set the hook, hoping it had been a musky's strike. But even though we hadn't even seen a musky so much as follow our bait to boatside, Pete was already plotting where he'd fish the next day. He's got that much confidence.

Pete has accounted for plenty of big muskies over the years, including another fish that cleared 40 pounds and a 41-pounder taken by a guiding client. He's quick to point out that his tactic is not for the angler looking to catch a bunch of muskies. "I figure that if I'm catching one fish for every ten days on the water with this technique, then I'm doing well. But you've got to remember that almost all the fish I'm catching are over 20 pounds," he said. "By fishing my way, it's rare to catch a musky that isn't at least in the 20-pound class."

Though Pete prefers the fall because he feels bigger muskies are more active then, he said deep water crankbait fishing is actually a tactic for any season of the year. While most musky anglers will keep their boat over deep water and cast to shallow weedbeds, Pete will do the reverse. It's not uncommon to see him with his boat parked atop the shallow weeds as he aims his casts toward deep water.

"I was schooled by people who fished the weedbeds for muskies. But while fishing with them, I couldn't help but think that while we were in 20 to 30 feet of water and casting to seven, the boat was floating right over the top of the bigger fish," Pete said. "Big muskies have to be somewhere and they have to be feeding somewhere, and if they aren't shallow, then they're deep. So why not fish for them there?"

Pete's theory is backed by the fact that many musky anglers

The weather may be cold, but Pete Haupt enjoys late fall as a prime time for catching big muskies from deep water lakes.

Despite snow in his boat and on the shoreline, and ice on half the lake, Pete Haupt continues his quest for a musky bigger than his 47-pounder of 1982.

in the fall will cast to shallow water while dragging suckers behind the boat as bait on an additional rod. Of course the boat is over deep water so the suckers are in deep water, and plenty of muskies are then caught on the large baitfish. "This is why people using suckers catch such big fish. It's not what the bait is, it's where the bait is. It's deep. I figured if I could put a lure down there in the same deep water and retrieve it in the same, slow, deliberate manner in which a sucker swims, then I could catch muskies on the lures just as readily as I could on suckers. And I was right."

Pete's reasoning didn't result in an overnight success for his tactic. In fact, it took him four or five years before he met with the success he had always figured he'd one day enjoy. "Fortunately, I stuck with it, and all of a sudden everything started to click. And it seemed all the muskies I caught were over 20 pounds, so I knew I was finally doing things right."

"Doing things right" to Peter Haupt means fishing exclusively in deep water with baits that will dive down to the depth the muskies are holding. Not content with many of the so-called "deep divers" offered by most tackle companies, Pete modifies his baits to fit his own style of fishing. Usually, that includes equipping the plugs with a larger diving lip, one that will create more water resistance and therefore push the plug deeper. A pipefitter and plumber in his younger days, Pete knows the value of different types of metal, and that's why his lures will often have a heavy brass diving lip to carry them even deeper.

Pete's quest for the ultimate musky crankbait led him to design the "Ojibwa" jointed plug, which sports a thick brass lip and, interestingly, only two treble hooks — one in the belly and one at the tail. "If there's one thing I hate it's when hooks tangle together and foul a cast," he explained. "With the hook placement as I make it, the hooks are far enough apart that they won't tangle, but when a musky grabs the bait he's not going to miss the hooks.

"One of the great philosophers of ancient times once said, 'Nobody ever missed a third eye.' If musky baits traditionally only had two hooks on them nobody would want one with three hooks on it."

Catching his 47-pound musky on an Ojibwa lure created an instant demand for the lure from other musky anglers. Pete marketed it for a few years, then sold out to Minocqua, Wisconsin, guide Dick Gries, who continues to make the bait under the name "Phantom Ojibwa."

A critical factor in retrieving any big crankbait, in Haupt's opinion, is to move it along slowly. A musky's metabolism is numbed by the cold water temperatures of fall, and it would be rare for a musky to move quickly to eat at that time of year. And a sucker's swimming pattern is slow to begin with, so Haupt feels his retrieve is a close imitation.

"I try to retrieve them as slowly as I can while still getting a wobbling action from the bait," he explained. "And sometimes I'll retrieve the bait irregularly, to give the image of a distressed baitfish, one that has faltered, lost its school, and is trying to get away to safety."

Pete's equipment is designed for fishing deep in cold weather. He uses 25-pound test monofilament because its thin profile allows his baits to dive deeper than braided dacron line. And he uses seven-foot-long fiberglass rods that have larger than normal-sized guides, which don't freeze up as quickly as smaller diameter guides. His choice of fiberglass for rod make is simply based on personal preference. "I don't know anything about graphite yet," he quipped. "When fiberglass came along, I embraced it and had no reason to change."

To combat the stress of cold weather on fishing gear, Pete uses baitcasting reels made by Ambassadeur "because they take the pounding of the heavy lures. They require no repair over the years."

Why big muskies are found in deep water is "one of the mysteries, the enigmas, of musky fishing," Pete said. Still, there are two factors he cited as being reasons why big fish will be found in the depths. One is the fact that most anglers fish shallow, so muskies in deep water don't get the pressure of their shallow water cousins. Secondly, he said, the food is better for muskies in deep water. Instead of eating crappies and perch in the shallows, deep water muskies have a high protein smorgasbord of ciscos, whitefish, suckers and even bullheads. "Crappies are like a potato chip to a musky, while a sucker or a bullhead is like a pork chop," Pete laughed.

"There is no doubt that there are many big, big muskies swimming around in the 'great ether.' They don't relate to anything but schools of baitfish, lying just outside the schools and only attacking when they're hungry. It's just that deeper lakes have such vast areas, that finding these fish is often like finding a needle in a haystack," Pete stated. "It's discouraging to try to find these fish sometimes, but they are wonderful fish to catch when you do find them because they're usually of a nice size."

Pete gave credit to the late Bob Ellis, a Vilas County, Wisconsin, musky angler, for getting him started thinking about

Pete Haupt tries to retrieve his crankbaits in an irregular and slow pattern, trying to imitate wounded baitfish that have lost their school.

fishing deep water. Ellis, as mentioned in Chapter Seven ("Trolling With Brian Long"), continued row trolling as an effective technique when its practice generally died out with the advent of modern fishing tackle. Ellis simply used the better rods and reels that became available but continued row trolling in deep water, and made some phenomenal catches. "He had the courage to just take off trolling in places nobody ever thought about fishing for muskies," Pete smiled. "He'd go trolling in 50 or 60 feet of water, looking for those same fish I'm looking for today. But he was the pioneer of this technique. What a guy."

Pete's preference for fall fishing is borne out by statistics that show that most big muskies taken in any one season are caught by the mere handful of anglers still on the water when October and November roll around. Colder weather signals big muskies to begin feeding heavily for the winter months, and Pete especially likes a weather change during this time — for better or for worse. "I really like to fish when there's a big snowstorm out in the Rocky Mountains. The muskies here will, for some reason, be on the feed. But I like days like today (30 degrees after a week of nothing higher than 20). The weather just seems nicer and the fish seem to know it," Pete said.

Pete's 47-pound musky, caught Oct. 27, 1982, came on just such a day. A strong southerly wind had melted the snow from a storm the week before, and rain fell periodically. Under identical conditions in 1981 Pete had lost a giant musky near the Penny Bar in Big Round Lake, and he couldn't help but think about that as he worked on a plumbing job. Finally, the temptation became too great and he snuck away, going back to his truck for a tool and never returning. He slipped his boat into Round Lake, and when he returned to Hayward that evening he brought with him the 54-3/4-inch, 47-pound musky.

Gubernatorial candidate Tony Earl was at nearby Cable for a debate with Republican opponent Terry Kohler, and recognizing a good photo opportunity, had his picture taken with Pete and his fish the next day. Earl won the election by a landslide, and Pete became an instant northwoods celebrity.

Pete concentrates on trophy waters only, lakes that have past reputations for producing big muskies. That's one of the reasons Big Round is his favorite, since it has produced giant muskies not only for Pete but for other fishermen. In the Hayward area, Big Lac Courte Oreilles, Whitefish and Grindstone also meet this criteria. "The lakes I fish generally have

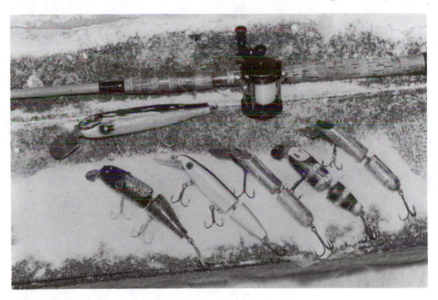

A sampling of Pete Haupt's favorite crankbaits include variations of original models, modified so they dive deeper than originally intended. The baits are: attached to rod — straight Pikie Minnow; and from left — jointed Pikie, jointed Bucher Depth Raider, Ojibwa, jointed Pikie, Ojibwa.

lower populations of muskies than the popular lakes, which get popular because they produce lots of muskies," Pete noted. "If a lake isn't popular, that further cuts down on the pressure the fish get, so that helps grow bigger muskies and preserve the ones that are already big. And when there's fewer muskies in a lake that means there's more food to go around to the available muskies. That means bigger fish."

The jury is still out on whether Pete Haupt will ever catch a bigger musky than his 47-pounder. It appears his deep water crankbait method is the right tactic. Now all he needs is to find the right fish.

Peter Haupt died May 20, 1994, after a long bout with cancer. If the muskies he's chasing now are bigger than those he chased on Earth, I hope God is his net man.

Chapter Eleven

Sucker Fishing with Steve Herbeck

"Hey! Hey! We've got open water!" Steve Herbeck's cheer rang through his Ford van as we topped the hill at the Presque Isle Lake boat landing.

Open water was an item of vital importance on that particular day, Nov. 17, 1991, thanks to an unusual cold snap that had gripped Wisconsin that year. Overnight temperatures had dipped into the 20s, and Steve's lake of choice, North Twin Lake in Vilas County, Wisconsin, had frozen shut just that night, probably for the winter, a full month earlier than normal.

Only two Vilas County lakes were still free of ice that morning — Presque Isle and giant Trout Lake. And Steve had his doubts about Presque Isle until he arrived at the boat landing, since surface water temperatures were around 34 degrees. Freeze-up was just days away.

"This lake is different from most lakes in that it is extremely deep, which keeps it from freezing for a longer period of time," Steve explained as he readied his big Skeeter boat. "North Twin is that way, too, but we lost it last night.

"Although I would have preferred to go to Twin because we probably would have had a couple of hits on the suckers and boated a nice musky or two, this lake could give us a whale. We'll probably only get one or two hits on our suckers out here, but our chances of sticking a 30-pounder in this lake are very, very good."

I had joined Boulder Junction, Wisconsin, guide Herbeck and his client for the day, Don Keck of Wisconsin Rapids, Wisconsin, on a late fall trophy musky hunt using a technique for which Steve has become very well-known — live bait rigging with suckers. Steve's background backs up his reputation — in 1987 he guided Jack Clifton of Stoughton to Wisconsin's largest musky of the year, a 43 pound six ounce brute from Lac Courte Oreilles near Hayward. Every year he has guided in Vilas County he has placed at least one fish in the top ten of the prestigious Vilas County musky Marathon. And during November of 1990, Steve and his clients boated 15 muskies of 25 pounds or better during a streak that baffles the imagination.

Don Keck was part of that hot string. "I fished with Steve for a couple of days and during that time we caught four muskies weighing from 20 to 25 pounds and I got a 32-pounder, which I released," Don recalled fondly. "One day we had so many hits on the suckers we figured the longest time we went between bites was 20 minutes. We seemed to always have a fish on."

Steve tried to explain why suckers are such a deadly bait on muskies, especially in the fall. "If you look at my records and the records of the Vilas County Musky Marathon and the records of almost any guide who fishes in the fall, you'll see that most of the bigger muskies are caught on suckers. These fish are very susceptible to live bait in the fall because they're feeding heavily prior to winter. And while they're wary to most other presentations because they've seen them hundreds of times from other fishermen during the course of the year, they know that suckers are good to eat. They just don't know that there is a hook attached."

Steve had checked with Don earlier to get his approval of my tagging along in the boat. Steve and I had made plans to fish together later in November, but the unusual cold snap, with some nights dipping below zero, had made us nervous. We feared the lakes might freeze over before we could fish together. Don had no objections, and even said that if I wished I could fish right alongside him and Steve. Any fish that hit Steve's or Don's line would be Don's to catch, but if a musky grabbed my sucker, it would belong to me.

Steve tied single-hook sucker rigs to our lines, then baited them with suckers measuring about 15 inches in length. About a foot and a half above the sucker he attached a one-ounce lead sinker. We were to lower the suckers to the bottom and occasionally lift them to keep them swimming as Steve slowly backtrolled into the wind.

Presque Isle, being a deep, clear lake with ciscos as a forage base for predators, is known for large muskies. It's also known for being notoriously tough to fish, but a lake that occasionally rewards a diligent angler with, as Steve calls it, a "whale." In about 32 feet of water off a rocky point, we put our lines into the water and Steve started backtrolling.

Barely 20 minutes had elapsed when I felt my sucker getting "nervous." Usually, a sucker will swim along with an occasional tug against the rod tip, but now the fish at the end of the line was pulling frantically. "Good," Steve said. "Maybe there's a big one down there following him and he's getting

Guide Steve Herbeck keeps an eye on his depthfinder while slowly backtrolling on Presque Isle Lake. Steve likes to keep the boat in 27 to 35 feet of water for this technique in late fall.

worried about being eaten. If you feel anything different, tell me."

The sucker stopped moving and then there was a heavy weight on the line. I lifted it gently, and instantly recognized the heavy yet slightly yielding weight of a musky. "He's got it," I said to Steve, and then he checked my line. "It's 'spongy.' You've got a fish."

Instantly Steve and Don brought the other lines into the boat and stowed the rods. I kept my thumb to the spool of the Ambassadeur reel, paying attention to what the musky was doing. It was moving slowly toward deeper water to where we hoped it would eat the sucker.

"Give me a time!" Steve asked Don.

"Nine twenty-five," Don replied.

"Let's wait him out," Steve said. There was an infectious edge to his voice. My hands trembled from the 25-degree cold and stiff wind, but my knees were shaking from the tension. How long we'd wait was up to the musky, so with nothing else to do but keep watch over the musky's actions, Steve and I talked about this technique.

Though using suckers as bait is largely thought of as a fall musky tactic, Steve told me that he's found it to be effective throughout the year. "June can be the best sucker month of the year. The muskies' metabolism is on the rise instead of on a decrease as in fall, and they have to feed. Boulder Junction taxidermist Al Smith had 13 trophy muskies (28 pounds or better) in his shop during this past June and nine had been caught on suckers. There's something to that," Steve said. "The problem is, people stop using suckers during July and August because it's almost impossible to keep them alive in warm water temperatures."

Steve starts using suckers when water temperatures dip below 60 degrees in fall, and has found they become especially effective when the water temperature is below 50 degrees. As the water cools muskies don't like to chase their food, and by November Steve and his clients will be fishing with suckers almost exclusively.

Early in fall Steve works suckers along the weed edges in 12 to 17 feet of water in lakes that have weeds, and 15 to 18 feet in lakes with little or no weeds. As the season progresses and the muskies move deeper, Steve will follow suit. In cisco-based lakes, Steve will move out to what he calls the "magic depth" — 27 to 35 feet. It is there, he feels, most big muskies will lie while hunting food.

Backtrolling — moving the boat in reverse while allowing baits to drag behind the boat — is legal throughout Wisconsin, and Steve uses this to his advantage. He will either use a three-horsepower Minn Kota electric motor or a 75-horsepower Mercury outboard to move his boat backward, depending on how strongly the wind is blowing. Though at times the 75-horse could move the boat at too fast a pace, Steve will use the power trim attached to the outboard to raise the propeller until it's barely under the surface of the water. "That will really slow you down," Steve explained. "Having that prop just under the surface allows you to creep along ever so slowly. And whether I'm using the electric or the outboard, I want the boat to move at a creep. It's just the right speed for working suckers in the fall. And backtrolling is the best way of controlling your boat. Moving the stern into the wind lets you keep the boat right where you want it."

Steve steers his boat in what he calls a "lazy S" pattern along any edge he can find, be it weeds or the rock bottom to mud bottom edge, since he believes muskies will use any edge as an ambush spot. He noted, "For big fish especially, work the rock-mud edge."

Besides looking for edges while watching his depthfinder,

Steve will also look for baitfish. He's a believer in what many guides call the "baitfish connection," which means that if there are baitfish present, muskies will be nearby. "But I won't put my suckers right in amongst the other baitfish because that's simply too much competition for my baits. Instead, I'll backtroll them below or off to the side of the schools of baitfish, trying to make them look like stragglers that would make an easy meal for a musky," Steve explained.

Over the years Steve has discovered certain hot spots that he calls "high percentage areas," where he's either caught fish before or has seen big muskies. These can consist of any inside turns in structure which tend to corral baitfish; points that drop into the deepest water in the lake; steep rocky shorelines that have some kind of wood cover; or any hard bottom mid-lake humps that rise up out of deep water. "It might be best to fish only one or two structures in a day's time if you have good spots. In the fall, muskies might only want to feed once or twice a day, so it pays to be on a high percentage spot when that happens," Steve noted.

As he steers the boat backward, Steve and his clients will bounce their sucker rigs along the bottom. He is a strong believer in a near-vertical presentation instead of simply dragging the sucker behind the boat. "A fisherman will get 70 percent of the hits in this manner as compared to a line that's just dragged behind the boat," he said. "By lifting the sucker off the bottom a foot or so every now and then you're keeping it moving, keeping it swimming above the bottom. You can feel when the sucker gets nervous...with the rod in your hand you can tell the instant something is different. And by bouncing the sucker rig's sinker instead of dragging it you'll get fewer snags."

So far, the musky at the end of my line was performing in what Steve called a "classic hit." It had grabbed the sucker in about 32 feet of water and moved out to 43 feet to eat it. As I checked the musky every minute or so, I could feel sharp tugs on the line, which indicated it was eating the sucker.

"I'd almost rather not have a wristwatch in my boat because I'd rather let the musky tell me when it's done eating the sucker. I asked for a time on this one because I want to be sure we get it. There are a couple of 40-pounders hanging around this spot that I and other guides have seen, and considering the way this fish hit it could be one of them. Plus, we've got to get a fish for pictures for your book," he laughed.

How Steve determines that a musky has eaten a sucker is

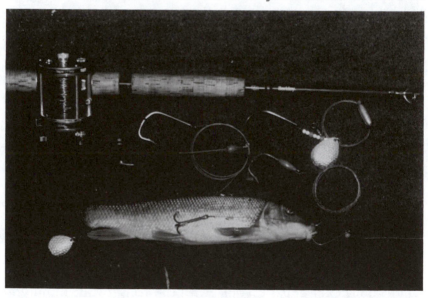

Steve's musky live bait rigs include large-gapped single hook rigs and quick-set rigs (as hooked onto the sucker). The Colorado bladed "tail gunner" imbedded in the gristle of this sucker and the spinner rig at the upper right are variations to traditional sucker rigs.

largely based on experience. "When they've finished eating it, they'll stop chomping on the bait and move off in a slow, deliberate pattern, or go right back to the same spot or depth where he grabbed the bait. When that happens, chances are he's got it," Steve said. "If a fish grabs a bait and never stops moving, either he swallowed it instantly or he's not serious about eating...he's just carrying it around. About all you can do when that happens is make the sign of the cross and set the hook and hope for the best."

The rig we were using, which is made by Bait Rigs of Madison, Wisconsin, and was designed by Steve, forced us to wait for the musky to eat the sucker because it consisted of a snelled, 14/0 square hook, filed razor sharp, and 100-pound test wire. Hooked through the upper lip of the sucker, it's not in a position to hook a musky until the fish turns the sucker to swallow it head-first. Steve uses these rigs almost exclusively in late fall because he's found that since muskies are so slow to grab a sucker at that time, less "rigging" on the sucker can mean more bites.

However, this rig is somewhat controversial in that it usually hooks a musky in the throat or in the stomach, possibly causing potentially fatal injuries to the fish. Steve doesn't believe in that, however. "Yes, you hook them deep, but it's a misconception that you're killing those fish," he said. "The thing to remember is to not try to remove the hook from the fish. Just cut the leader, and leave the hook in the fish. Its stomach juices will eat away the hook, and it'll be all right.

"I used to have a four-foot by four-foot aerated tank that I'd put fish in that I thought were marginal and might die because of the hooking job. Almost invariably, the muskies I'd put in that tank would be so wild after a couple of days that they were hard to get out of the tank to take back to the lake to release. I believe it's all in how you handle the fish. Just clip the leader, take a picture, and quickly release it back in the lake and that musky will be just fine."

Steve pointed out that his taxidermist friend, Al Smith, has told him that at least half the muskies brought into his shop that were caught on suckers were never hooked — the fish had swallowed the sucker and was brought to net without the hook ever penetrating the musky's stomach. "But, if you're still worried about it, use quick set rigs," Steve urged.

Quick set rigs have become extremely popular recently for this very reason. They consist of a single hook that is put in the lip of the sucker, and one or two treble hooks placed along the body of the sucker. Steve uses rigs with one treble hook, placing the treble along the sucker's side just in front of the vent. The theory is that when a musky grabs the sucker it will have the treble hook in its mouth and the angler can set the hook immediately, thus preventing a deeply hooked fish. Steve will use quick sets early in the fall and when he's had problems with muskies grabbing suckers on single hook rigs but not eating them, though they aren't his favorite rig. He feels they snag bottom and weeds too easily and impair the swimming action of the sucker.

On quick set rigs, Steve prefers using suckers measuring about 11 to 13 inches long. Still, on his single hook rigs he won't often use a sucker longer than 17 inches. "I will always choose vitality over size. My favorite sucker is a wild, black river sucker, rather than the 'gray ghosts' that have been kept in ponds all summer. A smaller but lively sucker will outfish a big, sluggish sucker anytime," he said.

Steve's equipment consists of either six-foot four-inch Berkley Series One or six-foot nine-inch St. Croix rods with Ambassadeur 7000 reels loaded with 30-pound test Trilene XT. "The 7000s have a greater line capacity than the usual musky reel, which will give me a chance if a fish wants to take line and I can't follow him because of motor trouble or some other problem. And the XT doesn't hold water or freeze to the reel like braided dacron line will," Steve explained.

He often modifies his sucker rigs, adding a large Colorado spinner blade and enough beads to the wire leader to keep the blade from slapping the sucker, or by pinning a snap swivel attached to a Colorado blade into the gristle at the bottom of the sucker's tail — a rig he calls a "tail gunner." The Colorado blade rig becomes especially effective with Steve's lift-drop vertical presentation, since each lift will start the blade spinning. "Either modification will cause a distinct thumping sensation when the sucker is swimming. Early in the fall, and especially in September, a spinner rig will outfish a straight sucker rig seven to one. But as fall progresses, the muskies want a more natural presentation, so I tend to stop using them then," Steve said.

Steve will fish every day of the season, but he's found an outstanding trophy time that has become a pattern from year to year. If a full moon occurs during the last week of October to the first week of November, bigger muskies will go on a rampage, he said. "That's when the big boys are caught, not just by me but if you check any records ever made of musky fishing. That full moon really seems to get the ciscos spawning, and the muskies just seem to act up at that time. And if I can get a drizzle or at least overcast skies with a southwest wind and 41 to 46 degree water temperatures during that time, watch out! Suckers die at that time! And that's exactly the conditions we had last November when I had such a good streak going."

As we talked, the musky indicated it had the sucker eaten — the chomping sensation I had been feeling had ceased, and the fish had moved back to the depth where it had originally grabbed the sucker. "What's the time?" Steve asked Don.

149

Guide Steve Herbeck hefts the author's 20-pound musky.

"Forty-five minutes."

"That's long enough. Reel down tight to the fish, and then set the hook hard," Steve directed.

Since Steve had positioned the Skeeter close to the musky the entire time it had been eating the sucker, it took little time for me to reel the line tight to the fish. When the line grew tight, I slammed the rod upward and felt a heavy weight as the fish came off the bottom.

Surprisingly, the musky didn't fight hard, perhaps because of the frigid water temperature. Quickly I brought it to net, and Steve unhooked it while in the net. "I think it will go about 18 pounds," he estimated, but then he lifted it from the netting. "Geez! Make that a solid 20."

The musky measured a shade over 40 inches long, but was

Steve Herbeck steers his big Skeeter boat toward the boat landing at day's end.

incredibly fat. Its distended belly indicated it had been feeding heavily. When I held it for a few quick photos, I had to agree with Steve about its weight; certainly it was one of the fattest muskies I'd ever seen. The musky was then released, and it strongly dove for the depths.

We didn't get our 40-pounder that day, or even a 30. But a 20-pound musky is still a trophy fish, and I was pleased with the way my season had ended. In a week I'd be deer hunting. But Steve wasn't finished — with 13 days remaining until the Wisconsin musky season closed on Nov. 30, he was going to stick it out as long as he could still find open water.

"I figure there's a 40-pounder still out there hungry for one of my suckers," he smiled.

To contact Steve Herbeck about a day of fishing, call him at (715) 385-2813.

Epilogue

Dec. 1, 1991

Wisconsin's 1991 muskellunge season closed at midnight last night, officially ending the quest of musky fishing fanatics everywhere to catch a musky bigger than they've ever caught before.

My season ended Nov. 17 when I left the water after fishing with Boulder Junction guide Steve Herbeck. Wisconsin's gun deer hunting season and a rapidly approaching deadline for this book kept me off the water the remainder of the month. Still, I could not fish much even if I had the time, for ice was rapidly claiming the musky lakes of northern Wisconsin.

Over the past six months this book has been a labor of love. It began May 7 when George Langley and I shivered in the snow squalls on Lac Vieux Desert, continued in 95-degree heat and high humidity on Teal Lake while fishing with Pete Maina, and ended among the skim ice floating on Presque Isle Lake in Herbeck's boat. Interestingly, I finished the year on the same note as I began it — I caught and released a 20-pound musky while under "Herbie's" tutelage, just a little bigger than the fish I put back while fishing with George.

It was quite a season. While writing this book I was able to see first-hand how some of the best musky fishermen in the

United States go about catching what some consider to be the fish of 10,000 casts. As a former fishing guide myself, I knew quite a bit about muskies when I entered the season, but as the summer progressed into fall I was amazed at how much more there is to know. Certainly each of the 11 guides I fished with knows more than could be contained within the 3,000-word format of the chapters of this book, but I tried my best to pass on as much knowledge as possible while making the chapters entertaining.

During the 11 days I spent on the water with these guides, six legal-sized muskies and two undersized fish were caught. Legal muskies were taken on four of the trips, as there were two days in which the guide and I each caught a fish. Every fish caught, from the two undersized fish to the 44-inch whopper I boated in August, were released in a healthy state. With luck, maybe I can tangle with these fish again. They are out there for you, too. That's the beauty of catch and release fishing — it makes fish a renewable resource.

I am sure I will be asked in the next few years which guide I felt was the best. To be honest, I really cannot say, for they are all good in their respective areas of expertise. I had as much fun (well, almost as much) fishing with Peter Haupt in early November when we didn't raise a single fish, as when I fished with Joe Bucher and we boated two very good muskies and a two-man limit of walleyes. Given different weather conditions and/or a change of luck, the situation could very easily have been reversed. I knew one thing — no matter who I was with, we were always working fish-holding water. All we needed some days was for the fish to cooperate.

What was drilled home to me again and again was the business-like way these anglers went about fishing for muskies. Their equipment was top-notch, their knowledge of the lakes first-rate, and their approach always analytical. For example, when a raucous wind prevented Dave Dorazio and I from properly working jerk baits, or when a clear-out cold front made surface baits a low-percentage technique when I fished with Roger Sabota, neither was above changing tactics to one that would work under the conditions. They played their best hands, so to speak, and by so doing proved themselves as top-shelf guides.

Many musky anglers will press a known guide for one or two "secrets" that will bring fish easily into the boat, or to tell them where on their favorite lake to go to catch a musky. The secret all of these guides have is diligence — years of being on the water, learning where to go and how to fish, given certain conditions. These men didn't get to be good through magic — they earned their knowledge through hard work and lots of time chasing what can be the most frustrating of all fish to catch. There is no secret outside of hard work.

I will be the first to admit I may have to change a method or two of how I used to go about musky fishing. I was constantly learning new or different retrieve methods, rigging practices, or fish location patterns that these guides have gleaned from lifetimes of being on the water, every day, for entire fishing seasons.

Never again will I have the opportunity to fish with such a group of knowledgeable musky anglers in just a year's time. Therefore, I intend to use this book as an item of reference, one that I will read and re-read as I try to become a better musky fisherman.

My one wish upon completion of this book is that its readers will be able to learn from it as I have learned from the 11 guides. If that is the case, then this book will have been a success.

About the Author

Steve Heiting is managing editor of *Musky Hunter* magazine and has written for nearly two dozen magazines covering the outdoor sports.

Heiting, of St. Germain, Wis., has been active as an outdoor writer since 1985. He is an officer of the Wisconsin Outdoor Communicators Association and an active member of the Outdoor Writers Association of America.

Musky Mastery: The Techniques of Top Guides is Heiting's first book, though he has written chapters for *National Forest Scenic Byways* (Falcon Press, 1990) and *Fresh Water Fishing Secrets* (North American Fishing Club, 1990) and edited *Fish Wisconsin* (Krause Publications, 1993) and *Surface Bait Subleties* (Outlook Publications, 1995).

Previously, Heiting served as editor of *Wisconsin Outdoor Journal* magazine for four years. In his spare time, he guides fishermen for muskies in Vilas and Oneida counties in Wisconsin and for smallmouth bass on Lake Superior's Chequamegon Bay.

A 1982 graduate of the University of Wisconsin-Stevens Point, Heiting has worked as an editor at newspapers in Ashland and New Holstein, both in Wisconsin. His former newspaper outdoors column, "Coming Out of Heiting," was honored several times by the Wisconsin Newspaper Association.

He and his wife, Connie, have three children.

Author Steve Heiting and friend.

The Fish...
The Flies...
The Fly Rod...

THE TROUT AT THE WALNUT TREE

By Richard Tate
144-pg., softbound
6"x9" size

$9.95

Join author Richard Tate as he spins trout lore, logic and experience gained from hundreds of hours on the stream into a book that's as entertaining as it is informative. Sure to be a quality addition to your trout fishing library.

Send your check or money order for $9.95 plus $1.50 shipping for each book ordered.

YOUR GUIDE TO WISCONSIN FISHING

Softbound / 8½"x11" / 224 pages / $15.00 retail

INCLUDES:

- Descriptions of 60 of Wisconsin's best fishing waters, details where and how to maximize your valuable fishing time...
- Over 50 lake maps showing depth and structure - A $75 value alone...
- Local fishing techniques, "hot" baits and the most productive areas to fish on each lake...
- Where to find local fishing information, bait shops, guide services, boat ramps and more...